A Dreamer's Travel Journal

How a 5½ week, 21 state #epicRoadtrip changed my attitude, my life and my health

JEAN TILLERY

KWE PUBLISHING

Tillery, Jean. *A Dreamer's Travel Journal: How a 5 ½ week, 21 state #epicRoadtrip changed my attitude, my life and my health*

Copyright © 2024 by Jean Tillery all rights reserved.

ISBNs: 979-8-9854135-2-6 (paperback), 979-8-9854135-3-3 (e-book)

Library of Congress Catalog Number: 2024907335

This story is dedicated to my mother, Suzanne Donahoe.

She was the person that I continue to strive to be. Her loyalty to friends and family, her love of travel and life itself, and her total commitment to her marriage and her faith are all things that I long to match.

I was adopted as a baby, and never for one moment did I question her love and acceptance of me and her belief that I was her child 100% through good and bad. It was because of that belief that I never questioned who I was. I never blamed my mistakes on not knowing where I came from. I never once said that my parents weren't my parents. I never once used my adoption as a crutch to justify my bad behavior or bad choices. It was also because of that I never really searched for information on my birth parents.

This story is as much hers as mine.

Mom...I miss you.

TABLE OF CONTENTS

Testimonials

I was so moved by the way you told the story. It just kept getting better. It is filled with times that evoke so many emotions. You capture some ot the deepest parts of our human experience.

I love the way the book flows. It made me want more and more. The songs you assigned each chapter just add another dimension to the experience. I will be reading it again and again.

   - Michele Marquis

Real, raw, emotional, and inspiring. *A Dreamer's Travel Journal* is a beautiful novel written about a cross country road trip and the ups and downs along the way. I'm in awe of the perseverance of the writer to keep going day after day even while dealing with some life-altering news.

I love how each chapter starts with song lyrics which

correlate with what the next chapter is about (adding several to my playlist now) and I also enjoyed the addition of the facts provided for the various landmarks along the way.

Reading this has made me want to plan an #epic road trip of my own!!

   - Angel Bolton

A Dreamer's Travel Journal is a marvelous book, filled with resources, information and insight. As with the best journey books, think *Travels with Charlie* by John Steinbeck and *The Hobbit* by J.R. Tokein, the places traveled to are less important than the experiences experienced.

I wholeheartedly reccomend this book for anyone, like me, who has ever dreamed...

   - Elizabeth A. Puett

Chapter 1

Opening

"Here's to the trains I missed
The loves I lost
The bridges I burned
The rivers I never crossed
Here's to the call I didn't hear
The signs I didn't heed
The roads I didn't take
The maps that I just couldn't read

It's a big old world but I've found my way
And the hell and the hurt lead me straight to this
Here's to the trains I missed"

"Trains I Missed"
Recorded by Walt Wilkins

Writers: Walt Wilkins, Nicole Witt, Gilles Godard

This book is different from most others you have seen. It chronicles the journey of an #epicRoad trip I took the summer of 2021. The story from what led me to take the trip… to when I finished writing the first draft of this book.

It is filled with journal notes, travel data and details, text messages, FB posts and lots of memories. It has a unique "organized disorganization" to it because that is the way I lived it.

While reading this story you will learn how much I love music.

It has been my therapy.

It has been my way to celebrate.

My way to motivate myself.

It has healed my heart.

It has healed my soul.

I am attracted to the songs that say what I can't.

At the start of every chapter are lyrics to a song. That song somehow speaks to what the chapter says. It may be one line…it may be the whole song. I hope that as you read about my journey, you will see how the song lyrics add to the story.

Some of the songs are old…some are by people you have never heard of…or if you have heard of them, you might not know that song. I have put all the songs on a Spotify playlist titled "A Dreamer's Travel Journal". Take a listen, I promise you will enjoy it and you just might find some new favorite songs.

Another thing that you will find different with this book is the photos. I have included only one picture with each chapter, but throughout this trip I took over 8000 photos. I have narrowed down that number to my most favorites and have stored them on my website to make them easier for you to see. Scan this to find them in files by chapters.

I also have a HUGE reference section. Way too much to print in this book, so each chapter has a reference list on my website. Check out all the details there.

And, like all my books, I want to know what you think.

Have you visited the places I did? Did you enjoy them?

Do you have questions? Comments? Complaints?

Reach out to me on my Facebook page or email me at jean@epiclivingwithjean.com

Chapter 2
Thank You

"Thank you for being a friend
Traveled down the road and back again
Your heart is true, you're a pal and a confidant"

"Thank You For Being a Friend"
Recorded by Andrew Gold

Writers: Lindy Robbins, Andrew Gold, Paul Blair, Rachel
Platten, Mark Nilan

Every adventure takes a bit of planning and sometimes, a whole lot of cash. I am not a newbie at fundraising, but I had never asked for money for a personal endeavor. It was painful and terrifying. To my knowledge, nothing had been done like this, so approaching people and asking them to PAY ME to drive across the country and fulfill a dream of mine seemed a bit nuts.

Yet, when I started to talk about this trip, what it meant for me and what I wanted to achieve, people agreed to join in the fun. For them, I am extremely grateful.

Originally this book was to be a Travel Journal of notes on my trip, places I visited, things that I saw, hotels that I stayed at, etc. It would mostly serve as a gift to the sponsors who believed in my vision.

The trip turned out nothing like I planned and in reality, turned out to be so much more. But I don't want to get ahead of myself.

There were four people that jumped at my request. They are businesses I work with a lot, people that I have come to know very well…and luckily…people who know ME well enough to know that this trip will end up being a wild adventure.

They Are:

Sharvette Mitchell of Mitchell Productions

Morgan Murray of Murray Automotive

Kim Eley of KWE Publishing

Melissa Blair of Cultivating Sales Pro

I am forever in their debt.

Find more information and links to each of them in the resource section of my website.

Chapter 3

Stop...

For Just One Minute

**"You don't have to guess what I'm against
If you know what I'm for"**

"What I'm For"
Recorded by Pat Green

Writers: Allen Shamblin and Marc Beeson

Before we continue, I have to say one thing. And this is a biggie. I am Catholic. God, and my faith in Him is front and center of everything that I do and therefore, He is the front and center of this story.

I am not trying to offend anyone. I am not trying to preach to anyone. I am not trying to judge, condemn, damn, or cast stones at anyone. Believe me, you will see, I am the biggest sinner there is, but my faith runs deep through this book. If that will disturb you, I sincerely ask you to put this book down. I am not into upsetting anyone. If you don't believe in God but are willing to look past all the faith references, I encourage you to keep reading. This story is a fun one if I say so myself. If you are a Christian, I pray that you see the hand of God in this story. Not only would I not be here without Him, but none of this would ever have happened without Him. I offer this up to His glory and I hope that you are not only entertained but inspired.

I am your average, everyday, married mom with three children. My kids are grown up and on their own and I have a business that I love that I can do from anywhere. I love my faith, my family and my friends. I battle with my self-esteem, my health, my weight and that inner voice that tries to sabotage everything I do. What I do have…a love of travel deeply instilled and nurtured by my parents. Especially my mom, who never met a backroad historical monument that she wouldn't stop at.

The other thing I have…is the Matthew Kelly book, *The Dream Manager*.

Chapter 4
Why

"Gotta little wild streak in my heart
I guess that I have had it since I heard the music start
I gotta little wild streak in my heart
I gotta little threadbare gypsy soul"

"Threadbare Gypsy Soul"
Recorded by Pat Green

Writer: Pat Green

I first heard Matthew Kelly speak in 2009. I was so motivated by what I heard that I went out and watched every video of his I could find and bought every book that he wrote. Matthew has a business consulting company called Floyd Consulting and through that company he developed the "Dream Manager Program". This program was designed to help businesses increase employee engagement, commitment and productivity by helping them to identify and fulfill their personal dreams.

Among the books he authored was a short little book called *The Dream Manager*. This book was a fable that described how the Dream Manager program would look when implemented using a cleaning company as the background.

At the time, I didn't have a business, but saw the potential in the Dream Manager program and immediately implemented the concept in my own life, and dragged along a few friends with me.

In a nutshell…the program starts with making a list of 100 dreams. Yeah. 100. Crazy huh? My first "Dream Group" made our lists, chose a long-term, a medium-term, and a short-term goal to focus on and then we would get together every few months and talk about our progress.

To say that it was a success would be a huge understatement. This program changed my life and the trajectory of my future. I know…sounds ridiculous, but it did. A simple little mind shift, a conscious thought about who you are, what you were created for, and a clear listing of what you really want to experience in your life changes everything. And I was hooked.

That was the start of it all, and for the last fourteen

years I have taken the last week of the year to look over my list, cross off what I completed, and remake my list of 100 dreams. Most of the dreams that weren't completed rolled over to the next year…sometimes I would eliminate dreams that I had outgrown or ones that just didn't seem to matter anymore. Some years, I was very focused on my list and conscious of making progress on my dreams, and other years I didn't do much with the list. That first Dream Group kind of fell apart, but I continued to make a list every year. And every year since the very first year, a cross-country road trip was on my list.

I had people ask me "Why" I want to drive across the country.

Why? Because I can.

Why? Because after being quarantined for over eighteen months I needed to get away. Big time.

Why? Because the media was using its voice to divide the people of our nation and were spreading a philosophy of anger and hate that I not only did NOT believe in...I did not agree that it existed everywhere.

Why? Because I believe that we have a culture and a people and a history that we should be proud of. We have not always gotten it right, but we have always tried to do better.

Why? Because many, MANY people do NOT have the means, the ability, or the desire to travel themselves to see the amazing people and places in our country.

According to the 2001 National Travel Survey, only 60% of the sixty thousand people interviewed traveled over 300 miles roundtrip that year. Only 5% traveled over

2000 miles. I consider it my personal mission to show them all the amazing things, big and small, that our nation has to offer.

AND

Why? Because I overheard a child say that they had no idea what Mt. Rushmore was, and I realized our kids are sorely lacking in the adventure dept and I wanted to set up a program to bring some of the people and places to them, (that is what I get for years of homeschooling my kids).

Those were just a few of the many reasons I wanted to take this trip, but the biggest reason was so that I could teach the world to dream.

During 2020…in the midst of Covid lockdowns…I came to realize that the Dream Manager program wasn't just for corporate employees…everyone needed a Dream Manager. Parents, teachers, kids, high school graduates, everyone.

I feel everyone needs to see how to become the best version of themselves by identifying and fulfilling their dreams, so I completed the process to become a Certified Dream Manager with Matthew's company. I then proceeded to adapt the corporate program to one geared to the people that I work with every day…in a small group setting so that it would be more easily attainable to anyone who wanted to join.

After all that work, I had to find the perfect way to launch MY Dream Manager program. Since my husband and I were heading back to Montana to visit friends I thought that was the perfect chance to fulfill that long-standing dream of my own, while I spread the dreaming message.

From the beginning, this trip was to be about work. All aspects of my business...not just dreaming, but #epic living and #epic cooking. And from there the planning began…

Chapter 5

Background

**"Sick and tired of being sick and tired
Everything around you is growin' old
The days drag on, the nights last forever
Every day's tougher just to keep it together"**

"Sick and Tired"
Recorded by Cross Canadian Ragweed

Writer: Cody Jay Canada

To get this story started, I really need to fill you in on some background information. It is tedious, but it is relevant in relation to the journey.

In February of 2021, I had Covid, but the story really starts earlier than that.

September of 2020 when I had surgery? Even before that.

Maybe in 2018.

2017?

Shoot even 2016.

And back to 2012.

And 2002.

Truthfully, I am not sure when exactly it started. Let's save us all some confusion and put it all in a timeline.

1999 My Dad died.

2000 I was pregnant and moved my mom from Houston, Texas, to Virginia to be close to me. When I packed up my two kids to fly down to Texas to be there when the movers came, she was in the hospital. When she came home from the hospital, I was taking care of a nine-year-old, a five-year-old, and a mother who was being ravished by cancer. All while packing up a two-story, three-bedroom house so that it would be ready for the movers.

2002 Mom died. Had to pack and sell her Virginia house. While taking care of a two-year-old, and homeschooling the other two.

2015 Perimenopause hits. I lose total control of my body and my mind. I stopped sleeping and started smoking.

Hormones had me on an endless emotional roller coaster. Mood swings were continuous and severe. I started gaining weight like never before and no matter what I did or what I ate I couldn't lose a pound. It's a problem that many women have around this age. Knowing that didn't help at all.

2016 The downhill spiral of physical and mental health continues until one night I wake up in the hospital. Now, I had never been much of a drinker. I seldom had a drink when I was just sitting at home, but when I went out I would. Especially if I was with my favorite road trip buddies. And especially if we were at a concert. Both of those were the case this night.

My husband and I and my two best friends had gone to Washington DC to see one of my favorite bands. I was looking forward to this show, as they had just released a new CD and I was excited to see a friend who worked with the band. There was a point during dinner before the show that I snapped. You never would have known. I was talkative and funny. Smiling and making jokes. All while oozing anger. The angrier I got, the faster I would down my drinks. The last thing I remember was two songs into the show being totally pissed off and wondering where I set my drink. The next thing I remember was waking up in the ER hours later. The story was that I had fallen down the concrete stairs at the venue and from the look of it, I landed on my face. The thought of which still mortifies me and makes me a bit ill. I am not sure if I fell and got knocked out or if I passed out then fell. Moral of the story is NEVER drink when you're mad. I can count on my fingers the number of drinks I have had since that night.

Nothing tastes the same. Mortification ruins everything. No one knew why it happened. I couldn't admit it to anyone. Never drink when you are angry.

I was very lucky. Although I was left with one side of my face black and blue and swollen, I didn't do any permanent damage. I had a major trip planned and a wedding for a close friend after that. Both of which I attended looking and feeling like the Phantom of the Opera. It took weeks, but the bruising and the swelling went away. I was left with nothing more than the memory of a horrible night, an overwhelming fear of losing control, and a scar on my face that not many people notice, but it is all I see when I look in the mirror.

After that night I was determined to move forward. I buried the humiliation and focused on forgetting that night and getting stronger and healthier. I joined the local CrossFit in May and for the first time in a long time, I felt better. For a bit.

2017 My health started spiraling back down again. For the first time being adopted and not having any family health history scared me. Hormones were still crazy, still couldn't lose any weight, and still lived on an emotional rollercoaster.

I had my very first panic attack on November 11th. I had no idea what was happening. I was driving home late at night after working a vendor show for my business and was sure I was having a heart attack.

2018 I thought I was doing better. And sometimes I was, though looking back, the downward spiral continued. I was getting so good at surviving that I didn't realize I was just "surviving" and not "living". The funny thing was, even with all this mental chaos, some of the most amazing things happened to me. My business was thriving. I stumbled upon the organization, eWomenNetwork and was chosen as the Managing Director for the local chapter. I loved working with other businesswomen, I loved working with Sandra Yancey the CEO of eWN. I was learning a lot and getting to do things and go places I never could have imagined. My kids were grown up and starting their lives.

I had my second panic attack on Christmas Day 2018. That fear that I had been carrying for so long turned to anger. Raw. Fierce anger. I was able to control it, but that control came at a cost. No one saw it. From the outside I had everything, while inside I was being eaten alive with resentment and self-loathing. I was moving forward and backward at the same time. It made no sense.

2019 January: I left CrossFit. I love the workouts and I loved the people, but I found it was getting harder and harder to push myself. I wasn't getting stronger, I wasn't improving, and it was taking longer and longer to recover between workouts.

By the end of the year, I had had it with being sick and I was ready to find out how to get better. I started working with a friend who was a nutritionist. The first thing she had me do was to take a DNA test. Since I was adopted and had no family health history, she wanted to see what type of genetic markers I had. This was all new technology for me, and I had never been interested in a DNA test, but my increasing concern with how bad I was feeling made me open to doing anything that would help.

2020 Donna went over my test results…DNA and blood tests. Not any good news. But news that was helpful to know ahead of time. I have a double marker for diabetes, a double marker for macular degeneration and was suffering from metabolic syndrome, hormonal disruption, insulin resistance and a myriad of other things. We developed a health plan, and that plan started with the big thing… having sinus surgery. I have always suffered from sinus and breathing issues. My earliest memories were of being about six years old and my mother trying to get me to take Dimetapp pills every night. I knew this surgery would have to happen someday but I always said I would put it off until I couldn't stand it anymore. Well, I couldn't stand it anymore. On top of that, I was pretty sure I was suffering from sleep apnea and there was no way to treat that until I could breathe through my nose.

In August I had a taste of just how bad I had gotten. The whole world was practicing social distancing. We figured the best place to stay six feet away from other people would be out West. Plans were made to head to Idaho to visit friends. From there we would spend a few days in Yellowstone with our son before heading to Montana to spend the week at Battlecreek Ranch for our fifth cattle drive.

Wearing a mask was difficult for me. Breathing was a struggle all the time…hitting the altitudes out west made it much worse. I was exhausted all the time. My husband and son would go walk at the stops in the park and I would sit in the car. And usually fall asleep.

Montana was no better. I was in no shape to ride. I would get up for breakfast with everyone and when they took off on the horses, I would go back to bed.

It was then I realized that it was time. Time to talk to a surgeon about surgery on my sinuses. I have had breathing issues my whole life, I knew that surgery was going to have to happen at some point and I had hit that point.

September 2020 was the surgery. The doctor said that one side of my nasal passage was almost 100% blocked and the other was 90% blocked. Usually this procedure is outpatient, but because he had to do so much cutting, he wanted me to spend the night in the hospital for observation. I was miserable, but the thought of being able to breathe again, and maybe actually having some energy to MOVE was what kept me going.

October 2020, ten days after surgery I had my follow-up appointment and the surgeon was quite proud of how well it went, and how well I was healing. The splints were removed and I was cleared to start working out again as long as I kept the weights light and didn't do any jumping or running. Fine with me…

I left the surgeons and hopped on a plane for a quick trip to Texas for a mastermind meeting. Two days later when I got back on the plane to fly home, I was starting to have problems catching my breath. I was certain I overdid it. When we landed in Richmond, I struggled to get off the plane. Walking up the jetway took more energy than I had and although my nasal passages were open and clear, and I wasn't stuffed up, I couldn't breathe.

I had to stop and sit to catch my breath when I finally got into the airport. I had to sit and rest two more times before I got to baggage claim. Y'all…our airport is not that big. I was scared. This is not what I expected to feel like.

The surgeon told me that I would feel like a new person and that things would be 100% better and yet, I was much worse.

I had bought a blood oxygen reader months ago when I started to have problems with breathing and energy…and I was startled by how low my O2 levels would drop after any exertion at all. Going up the stairs, walking even the shortest distances, even washing my hair too aggressively would cause it to drop to 85% and sometimes even lower. It never stayed down long which was good and I learned how to stop and focus on my breathing until it came up again.

I apologize for this long-drawn-out chapter. I wanted to cut it out altogether, but I needed you to see the state I was in, and why this trip was such a stretch for me. The sad thing is…I hear the same story from other women. My story is not unique. At least up to this point.

Chapter 6

Covid

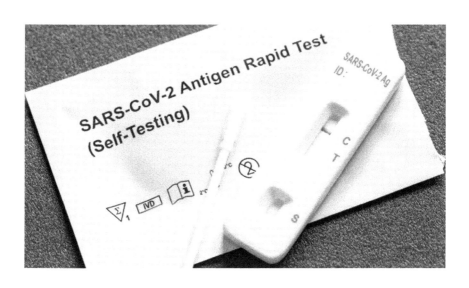

"I'm just praying, praying I make it through the night"

"The Night"

Recorded by Morgan Wade

Writers: Michael Joseph Wise, Morgan Dealie Wade, Sadler Jennings Vaden

In January 2021 my oldest came in from Texas to visit. All our plans for fun while he was here got canceled when we learned that a co-worker he had been with had tested positive for Covid. Within 4 days, he, my husband and myself all tested positive.

I am not sure which "variant" we had, but luckily, none of us got very sick and none of us needed to be hospitalized. I think one of the things that helped us was that I was already working with Donna, and as a health practitioner, she was prepared. The minute I found out that my son had been exposed I contacted her and she sent me her Covid protocol with a shopping list, instructions and things to watch out for.

Since Covid likes to hit you at your weakest spot, and I already was having oxygen problems, we focused a lot on keeping my lungs healthy. Breathing treatments, nebulizers, extra supplements geared to help my lungs. What I wasn't prepared for was the mental attack that Covid would have.

Dan and I had plans to head to Texas for a Courtney Patton and Jaime Lin Wilson show. We were scheduled to leave Feb. 18th so we were watching the calendar closely when we tested positive on Feb 1st.

We each quarantined in different areas of the house. For me, Covid was like having strep throat. Slight fever, but mostly just a sore throat and tired. At least for the first 2 days. After that, I hit a stage that was the worst I have ever felt in my entire life. I was exhausted to a point that I almost couldn't function physically and mentally I was falling apart. I was sleeping 18 hours a day and crying the other 6. I had a problem with doing anything that required thinking and was making mistakes and forgetting things left and right. I couldn't wait to get past this and back to normal. I had no idea that 'normal' was gone forever.

Covid changed me. More than the "covid brain" that people talk about. It changed my personality and that scared me. For the first time ever, I was sure I was going to die. Absolutely sure. And that bothered me. My whole life I dealt with having no family health history with the acceptance that whatever happens…happens, and I would deal with it. I wasn't looking forward to death, but I wasn't afraid of it. Not knowing never caused fear or uncertainty.

During those days with Covid there was no uncertainty because I was certain that this was the end. And I WAS afraid. And that pissed me off. I remember wondering why all of a sudden I was filled with fear. That was not like me at all.

As the eighteenth got close there came a new problem. Texas was slated to have a massive ice storm. We were worried about getting Cody back to Houston before the storm hit. Luckily, he made it back hours before the ice started and the power went out.

We were able to fly to San Antonio on schedule after the storm abated and the power returned. It was also just in time to show me what life after Covid would look like.

I thought I had low energy and oxygen levels BEFORE Covid, that was nothing like I had after. In San Antonio, we tried to walk around the city, but I couldn't go more than ½ block before I would be too tired to continue. From San Antonio, my husband went to South Texas to fish with my brother and I headed to Tomball Texas to see a favorite musician play at my favorite venue. I had tickets for two nights. Except for going to the shows, I never left my bed in the hotel. My mental state was getting worse and worse. I kept wanting to care about…anything, but caring took too much energy.

I saw my doctor who immediately freaked when she heard how low my O2 levels were still going. She wanted me to go to the hospital, but I promised her that if it stayed low I would go immediately. She ran some heart tests and saw that the left side of my heart was enlarged and she was concerned about what else could be going on. She scheduled me with a pulmonologist and a cardiologist. Both of which ran every test they had. They were seeing problems but had no real "diagnosis" for me. Both of them slapped me with several prescriptions and said come back in 3 months.

The only positive out of it all was that my sleep study did show that I was stopping breathing 93 times an hour. No wonder I couldn't sleep through the night.

April brought in our yearly music festival in Key West. This was the 4th year, and usually it was held at the end of January but this year, because of Covid, it was pushed back. This festival is usually the highlight of my year… but this year I spent 90% of the week in bed. I did make a couple of the night shows but couldn't do more than sit in my chair. I was worse than miserable; I was irreparably broken. I no longer cared if I died, in fact, I often thought that if I was dead then I could just keep sleeping.

My life continued only because I forced myself to keep moving. My mornings weren't too bad, but by lunchtime I was too exhausted to work, often falling asleep at my desk. I had to quit driving after noon because I would fall asleep WHILE I was driving. And I don't mean "nodding off while sitting at a red light…I am talking about waking up in the wrong lane going 60mph. I was usually in bed by 4:00 pm, and if I was lucky, I would be able to wake up about 8:00 pm for an hour or so.

At some point in the middle of this hazy time, I got the wild idea to drive across the country. We decided to go back to Montana for the 2021 Cattle Drive and I figured why not drive there? I mean, it makes sense right? Not sure what kind of health issues could pop up. Unsure of how many hours a day I could drive. Not sure if I could handle it mentally.

One thing I was sure of, for the first time in a long time, I had something to look forward to. Something to work for. The planning began.

Chapter 7

Holy Water
and
Hand Sanitizer

"Be prepared, be prepared
This lesson must be shared
This lesson must be shared, be prepared
Be prepared, be prepared
And unless you got a spare
You got one life so handle it with care"

"Be Prepared"
from the movie Hoodwinked

Writer: James Todd Edwards

Are you a planner? I am a planner. I got that from my mom. I love the time I spent planning, organizing, and thinking through the trip. This was necessary for several reasons.

1. I was going to be gone for a long time.
2. I had many different events to be prepared for, all needing very specific clothes/tools, etc.
3. I had a whole lot of work stuff to accomplish while I was on the road.
4. I had no idea how my health was going to hold up from day to day.
5. I had a vague overview of the route I would take and the sights I wanted to see, but I was going to have to continue to do research every day and try to stay a few days ahead of schedule.

This is not normally how I would suggest handling a vacation, but my thought was that this was a business trip. I was going to go across the country and spread the message of "healthy eating" and "finding your dreams".

The first stop was AAA. If you travel…for ANY reason, you need to have a AAA membership. I didn't end up needing it on this trip but over the 40 years I have been driving I have used it often. And not JUST for when I lock the keys in the car.

When I was younger and we would go on family trips, my mother would always have AAA design a "Triptik" for us. Back then it was a flip-style map that ran top to bottom with the road you were taking. They aren't really needed today with modern GPS on your phone, but when I stopped by AAA to pick up maps and Tour books, the lady helping me asked if I wanted one and I said heck yeah... for old times sake. When she asked where I was going, I said Montana and back. Starting in VA and going through WV, MD, PA, OH, KY, IN, IL, WI, MN, ND, SD, WY, MT, ID, UT, AZ, NM, TX, OK, AK, MS, and TN. I think I scared her.

The next stop was Google.

Years ago, long before GPS on your phone, I was coming home from my summer conference and I took a back road and got a little lost. I knew which direction I needed to go and figured I would get home sooner or later. The first thing I ran into was a wind turbine farm. Now, coming from Texas, I am not unfamiliar with wind farms. Down there they are mostly located on flat land and are set up in a grid pattern. Lined up in rows...row after row. Here, they were situated on the top of the mountains and follow the ridge lines. One long row. As you are traveling along the mountain roads, they come in and out of sight. It is like playing hide and seek. I remember when I stopped for gas, the station was right across the street from one of the turbines. I had never seen one close up, and this girl was geeking out.

The other thing I saw on that trip was a huge mountain "crag" in the distance. I had no idea what it was, but it reminded me of what I saw in Colorado and Montana. When I got home and told my husband, he knew exactly what I was talking about and told me that it was called Seneca Rock and had some of the best rock climbing in the state of WV. I decided that someday I would go back and see it close up. Not to climb. Just to see.

My #epicRoadTrip was that chance, and as I planned

my first stop of the trip…the summer conference at Franciscan University, I knew I had to backtrack the way I came home all those years ago. Problem was, I had NO idea where that was. Thank goodness for Google. I was able to find where I had been and routed my trip that way. I was able to loosely piece together the entire five and a half weeks based on what I wanted to see. I decided to take the most northern route. That would give me the opportunity to see as many family and friends as I could squeeze in, as well as be able to hit North Dakota, one of the few states I had yet to visit. I also decided to leave a few days early so that I could spend some time in Pittsburg before heading to my conference in Ohio.

There is nothing as exciting as sitting down and Googling "the best things to do in…"

I had a list of 20 things I wanted to do in Pittsburgh. I broke them down by "have to do", "really want to do", and "it would be cool to do". A day and a half was not going to be near enough time.

I made an outline of what I wanted to do in Pittsburgh but didn't really get into details for the other places that were on my travel itinerary. My biggest problem was with the lingering health issues I had, I wasn't sure how many hours a day I could drive. Heck, I wasn't even sure I could finish the trip, even if my doctors cleared me to take it.

That was the next hurdle. My doctors were surprisingly encouraging about the trip. We had backup medical forms and prescriptions, backup plans if there were problems, and an extraction plan if everything went south. My cardiologist recommended getting a temporary handicap parking permit, but I refused. I promised to be responsible, stay on top of my health and all my medications, and make sure that I was aware of how I was feeling at all times. And with that promise, I had the blessings from both of them.

The next step was planning on how to pay for this trip. This is a HUGE undertaking. Since it was a business event and I am all about the marketing, I decided to get sponsors for the trip, so that meant developing a sponsor strategy and information packet. As I talked to people and shared my vision for this trip, I did get sponsor money, but I also got more excited and got even more ideas. I took a notebook and started planning, setting goals, creating guidelines, budgets, lists, lists and more lists.

I worked with Sharvette Mitchell, a marketing genius who helped me fine-tune my plan, worked with me on social media strategy, and even taught me the ins and outs of how to do it. I had a designer create logos, help me to research marketing and promotion products.

I worked with my CRM company to develop systems to maintain my business while I was on the road, but to also streamline individual donor capabilities and ways to keep in contact with them.

I thought I would do promotion along the way and started looking into media outlets to contact and groups that I could talk to about the Dream Manager program.

I needed a team to support me, to keep me motivated and on track, so I started making lists of people to ask to help. I wanted to share my passion for travel and adventure with kids, so I developed a "Kids Club" that would correlate with the trip and wrote tons of content to share with them and planned specific places to do live broadcasts from. I planned for videos to be done along the route and wrote daily content to be used.

And if that wasn't enough, I had to figure out exactly how I was going to live on the road for that long. What I needed to take, and how I would get it all in my car. The first hurdle was the fact that I had 4 periods that would need specific clothes and tools for.

1. The Defending the Faith conference. I would be staying in the dorms on campus so that meant, fan - check, towels and extra pillow– check, notebooks and book bag–check.

2. Midway through the trip, I was meeting my husband in MT for a cattle drive. I need his pre-packed suitcase with clothes and riding gear–check, his fly fishing gear–check.

3. The eWomenNetwork ICON conference in Dallas. I need dress clothes and shoes. I had a photo shoot planned while there so I need clothes and props for that.

4. My general travel clothes, products and supplies for cooking classes, 2 cases of Dream Manager books, marketing material, food and water, computer, podcast and photo gear…

This is where the most detailed planning happened. I bought 6 big, clear, plastic tubs and had them set out on my dining room table and started thinking through each stage of the trip. This is how it all worked out.

- I had one bag with all my meds, my everyday basic care routine items and general makeup. This would come into the hotel with me every night, along with my computer and whatever clothes I needed for the next day.

- I had one suitcase JUST for the eWN conference, and one JUST for the DTF conference.

- Everything else was packed in tubs. One for shoes and seldom used clothing. One for shirts, one for bottoms, one with electronic supplies, one with cooking class supplies and one with marketing and misc supplies.

- I had a medium size cooler for food, and a small cooler for re-fillable water bottles. Everything had a designated space in the car and believe it or not, it all fit. I was able to get to what I needed when I needed it. It was glorious. I NEVER would have imagined I could live for so long, with so little stuff.

The next thing I put together was my PDR binder. That binder is a trick I learned from Sandra Yancey, CEO of eWomenNetwork. PDR stands for Plan-Do-Review. All my pertinent travel information went into that binder. Trip details, contact information, schedules, Dan's flight details, Routes, and emergency information.

That binder was with me the whole trip and I would make notes about what worked and didn't work, what I did, saw and experienced. What I forgot to bring and what I wished I had thought of.

When the trip was over, I sat down with the binder and went over all my planning, and doing, and outlined what I would change if (when) I did this again.

July 25th, the Sunday before I left, I flagged down Fr.

Espinoza, a visiting priest after Mass. Father is from our sister parish in Quito Ecuador. For the last 20+ years our parish has been sponsoring a daycare and educational center at his parish, and each year he comes to Powhatan to visit and to bring updates about the school. He has become a very dear friend to me over the years.

I asked if he could please give me a prayer and a blessing for not only safety on my trip but for good health to see it through and for my message to be heard and to bear fruit, which he did. Then he also added this. A prayer asking God to open my heart to the new and wonderful gifts He had for me and to stretch my understanding of His purpose for me. At the time, I had no way of knowing how powerful and prophetic that prayer would be.

Last things on my packing list...my protection items. A large bottle of hand sanitizer and a larger jar of Holy Water.

Chapter 8
Let's Go

"And I can feel the wind
Blowing against my skin
How long has it been?
I don't know
Since I've felt alive behind the wheel"

"Open Road"
Recorded by Drew Kennedy

Writers: Josh Grider and Drew Kennedy

Day 1: Wednesday, July 28th   9:31 AM

There is something very anti-climatic about finally getting into the car and hitting the road. All this planning and no "celebratory" send-off? Just a picture with my husband in the garage as we say goodbye. See you in a few weeks. A quick picture of my mileage for reference. Reset the trip miles to 0. And hit the road.

Of course, as usual, I have a few stops to make on the way out. Library books to return. Stop at the post office, the bank and the Powhatan Chamber of Commerce office. That worked out in my favor because I got a speaking gig for when I got back. I will be leading a book study on "The Dream Manager". I am not even on the road yet and I am spreading the Dream message. It won't be long before I earn the title of "The Crazy Dream Lady"

Two hours to Harrisonburg, Virginia. If I wasn't in such a hurry, I would stop and see my son. I remembered to do something at the start of the trip. Something I learned from my mother, that she did EVERY single trip we took. I used to do it when my kids were younger, but somehow, I got out of the habit. I said a prayer as I got on the road after running my errands. As I merged onto Highway 64 heading West, I once again prayed the words that Father Espinoza said a few days before. Please keep me safe. And healthy. And open-minded.

I love driving West through Virginia. It isn't long down the road until you start seeing the mountains ahead of you. I have been out in the Western United States plenty of times, the mountains there put ours to shame…but there is something about them I still love.

Some people are beach people…and don't get me

wrong, I love the beach, the salt air, the pounding of the waves, the endless horizon, the sounds of the birds and the treasures that get washed up in a high tide. But it is the mountains that I feel call me home. The timelessness. The power. The hard edges, the fierceness. The struggle. The stillness. The soft echoes from places long ago and far away. The wildlife. Our mountains may not be as big or tall or grand but those same feelings exist here.

If you ever get the chance, take a drive on the Blue Ridge Parkway. The parkway is a National Parkway known for its beauty. It is America's longest linear park and runs 469 miles linking The Shenandoah National Park to the Great Smoky Mountains National Park through Virginia and North Carolina.

You won't get anywhere quickly, but there is a beauty there like no other. Especially in the fall.

Another one of the BIG dreams on my Dream List is to hike the Camino de Santangelo. There is a group of us who have been talking about it for years. Before Covid, I had actually developed a "training schedule" to prepare us for that trip. One of the items on the schedule was to spend a few days hiking the Appalachian Trail. For those up to the challenge, the trail follows closely with stretches of the Blue Ridge Parkway through Virginia.

Virginia is still very agricultural, and that shines in the western part of the state. Horse farms, apple orchards, and of course, vineyards are sprinkled throughout the area, but my route today takes me through lots of cornfields. Beautiful farmhouses and tiny farm towns.

I am driving in silence which is not at all normal for me, but the quiet in the car brings peace. Although I am a little apprehensive about the trip…I can feel the excitement starting to build.

Chapter 9
West Virginia

"Almost heaven, West Virginia"

"Country Roads"
Recorded by John Denver

Writers: Bill Danoff, John Denver, Taffy Nivert Danoff

Still Day 1: Wednesday, July 28

Two things to notice as you get close to the state line from Virginia into West Virginia. The road gets curvier, and you lose internet. As you get into West Virginia, there is a beautiful roadside viewing area overlooking the Germany Valley. It is high in the Allegheny Mountains and was originally settled by German farmers in the mid-18th century. The parking area isn't huge, but I was the only one stopping today. The sky was clear and the view was fantastic. There was a historic marker there that tells a story involving Seneca Rocks, where I was heading, and two brave resourceful women. I have to admit, one of my favorite parts of the stop was looking at all the stickers that people had put on the guard rails. They were from everywhere!

I turned off the main road onto Route 9 that would take me to Seneca Caverns and found my first detour. Being a history buff, one of the places I like to stop at when traveling is the local cemetery. I know that is a little creepy, but there is so much information on the tombstones. You can find so many stories and trace them through families by the stones.

The North Fork Memorial Cemetery caught my attention because it was off the main road, at the top of a hill. The backdrop to the headstones were the mountains that surrounded it. What a majestic spot to bury your loved ones. There was a tall flagpole in the middle, and on that day, there was just enough wind to keep the flag fluttering. It stood out proudly against the blue sky and white clouds as if to say, I am an important place. I took a few moments to wander among the graves finding families and wondering about the stories, like the mother who lost a son when he was eighteen, just to lose her husband ten years later. I wonder how she felt for the next thirty years of living without them both.

It was such a perfect day, such a quiet place, I could have spent more time there…but I had places to go, people to see, and I had been waiting for my next stop for years.

Before I get to Seneca Rocks and Seneca Caverns, I want to point out another lesson that I learned from traveling with my mom. We used to tease her about there being no roadside historic marker she wouldn't stop at. Well, she must have been in Heaven looking down and laughing at me, because during this part of the trip, there were three that I had to stop at, (in my defense, there were actually a couple I DIDN'T stop at).

The first one was this huge stone carved into an arrow point. It told the story of John Justice Hinckle and the block house he built there which later became the nucleus for a colonial fort, and later, during the Revolutionary War, was called Fort Hinckle.

The second, on the way out of Seneca Park, was a marker attached to a huge stone, flanked by the American Flag on one side and the West Virginia flag on the other. This one caught my attention because the marker said "Battle of Riverton". My husband lived in a house on Riverton Rd in West Lafayette when we were in college so I had to get a photo.

The last one was actually at the Seneca Rocks Center. It was dedicated to the 10th Mountain Division who had trained at Seneca Rocks for the mountain warfare they would face in WWII.

Before I continue, I have to say something. I know the trend lately is to try to erase our history. To sand down the edges so we can ignore the people we don't like. Those who held beliefs we don't agree with. Who did things that today we view as wrong. My problem with that is, in that process we also negate the sacrifice of the people who were doing good, and we eliminate the good that was done by people who may have been not always so good. Our history is our history. We need to take the good and the bad. Without knowing where we have been, we will never know how far we have come, and see why it is important to keep getting better. As a country, we may not always get it right, but I believe as a whole, we are good people, all yearning for the same thing. A chance to build a better life for our families in a place where we are free to live the life we choose to live. These historical monuments reflect the people who felt strong enough to fight, and sometimes lay down their life, for that belief. We need to remember. To honor, and maybe to do better. But we can't ignore it.

Now off my soapbox and down the road. I stopped first at the Seneca Caverns. As I walked into the gift shop that sold tickets for the tour, the lady at the desk was on the phone with a group arriving on a bus who would fill up the spots on the next tour. I didn't want to wait around for the tour after that one, so I popped up to Ashbury's Restaurant, which is onsite, and got a bowl of ice cream. Yes, that was my lunch. Not very healthy but a celebration of sorts. I ate it on the front porch overlooking the mountains. I still had a sort of surreal feeling about the trip. I was excited, but still so unsure of how I would feel. I was ready to face whatever came.

Just a few minutes down the road and I was able to catch my first glimpse of the distinct rock formation that is Seneca Rocks. It is stunning from a distance, but as I got closer it was even grander. There is a Seneca Rocks Discovery Center at the base of the mountain. They were closed that day, and I was a little upset about that, but the benefit was that there were very few people around. The back of the discovery center is a huge viewing porch with a spectacular view of the face of the rocks. The information board said that the first recorded ascent was in 1939, but now you could take one of the over 400 routes up the mountain. It is the most popular climbing spot on the East Coast and climbers come from all over the world to climb it. The sign showed the 22 most popular trails. The easiest being a 1.5-mile walk to the observation tower. The other trails were coded as moderate climb, difficult climb, or extremely difficult climb. I would have loved to be able to do the easy trail. 1 ½ miles normally would be no problem at all, but in my delicate health, it was a concern. That, and the fact that it was very hot and there were not many people around. I was worried about getting stuck on the trail somewhere and losing too much time. I promised myself I would be back someday to hike it.

After leaving the 'discovery' center, I soon 'discovered' the problem that would haunt me the entire trip. While I was enjoying my ice cream at the caverns, I tried to do a live video and realized that internet connection was going to be an issue. It became an even bigger problem after leaving Seneca Rocks because I also lost my GPS and my cell coverage. Good thing I had my AAA trip-tics. Except…the new trip-tic routes were not like the old ones. They were nothing more than maps printed off an online

"Mapquest" type of program. I had NO idea where I was because nothing was labeled. You can't figure out which way to go if you didn't know where you were starting from. I also realized that my daughter was supposed to call me. She had a meeting with the venue where she wanted to have her wedding. Dad was filling in for me since I was gone, but she was going to call when they had a date worked out.

I found myself praying that there were no problems she needed me for. I was going to be totally unreachable. For how long, I didn't know. I was a little uneasy but thought, what the heck. I made it through this area years ago, I can do it again. I really had no time restraints so I continued down the road enjoying the view. And the extremely winding roads. I mean really winding. With some pretty steep inclines. Luckily, there was still little traffic, and for the most part, I had the road to myself.

I wanted to take video from the camera mount I hung in my car, but the roads and the turns were so tight, you really couldn't get a feel for how extreme the drive was.

It wasn't long until I first spotted the OTHER reason, I took this route. As I headed North, I got in range of the Mt. Storm Wind Farm. Like I mentioned earlier in the book, for some reason I am totally mesmerized by the sight of these massive turbines on top of the mountains. Then I found myself at the gas station I discovered the last time I went through this area. It was the perfect time because I needed a bathroom and gas, and at that moment I got cell coverage back and Hannah called. The wedding date was set, my car was full of gas and I was back on the road.

Through West Virginia, a few miles of Maryland, and then into Pennsylvania. Making great time. And feeling great!

Chapter 10
Pittsburgh

"And it's a great day to be alive
I know the sun's still shining
When I close my eyes
There's some hard times in the neighborhood
But why can't every day be just this good"

"It's a Great Day to Be Alive"
Recorded by Travis Tritt

Writer: Darrell Scott

Day 2: Thursday, July 29

The song lyrics I chose for this chapter are from Travis Tritt's song, "It's a Great Day to Be Alive".

I chose that song because after waking up on day 2… that is exactly how I felt. It finally hit me…the sheer magnitude of what I was starting. I was surprised the drive yesterday hadn't tapped me more than it did. I think all the stops and the moving around in between really helped.

I got into the Pittsburgh area, but knowing very little about the city I made the call to stay a little further out, away from the city center. I have traveled a lot and there have been times in cities that I found myself not very comfortable in the area I was staying in. I got in and settled and slept very well. I woke up ready to take on the world. Or at least Pittsburgh.

I planned on spending the whole day seeing the sites on my "must-do" list, but then I would also have a few hours in the next morning to do some more.

I have to tell you about this hotel room. It was a bit bizarre. It was a large room for a mid-value hotel. It had a seating area that had a huge soaker tub. The tub was kind of in the room and kind of in the bathroom, you will have to check out the pictures. It was the shower that I loved though. It was like one you would find in an ultra-modern home. All tile, and huge. It had a bench, a wall shower head AND an overhead shower head. I have never seen that in even some of the luxury hotels I have stayed at.

My pre-planning paid off this first day…there were 3 things on my list. I had gotten free tickets to watch the Steelers training camp…I wanted to see the Duquesne

Incline and Randyland. Sounds like fun huh? Well it was!

First up was the Incline. It is a cross between a street car and an elevator. It was originally designed to carry cargo up and down Mt. Washington but later carried passengers, mostly serving the working-class people who were forced out of the low-lying riverfront area by industrial development. Originally there were inclines located all over Mt. Washington, but as better roads were built and auto use increased all the inclines were closed but the Duquesne Incline and the Monongahela Incline.

In 1962 the incline was closed but local Duquesne Heights residents launched a fundraiser and it reopened under the management of a non-profit organization dedicated to its preservation. It has since been totally renovated, the cars have been brought back to their original wood and an observation deck at the top was added. It is now listed on the National Register of Historic Places and is one of the city's most popular tourist destinations.

The ride up the side of the mountain goes a whopping 4.3 mph, so that gives you time to admire the view as you climb up an elevation of 400 feet at a 30-degree grade. When you get to the top, the observation deck gives you a view of Pittsburgh's "Golden Triangle". The Golden Triangle is the downtown center of Pittsburgh where the Allegheny River and the Monongahela River join together to make the Ohio River. This area features offices for major corporations and is where many of the industrial barons made their fortunes.

Across the river I could see my next destination… Heinz Field, but first some lunch. The area at the top of the Incline was very trendy and there were a lot of cool places to eat. I chose the closest place as I was starving. I didn't have a lot of time and I was getting a little worn out and wouldn't be able to walk far. Oh, it also started raining. Luckily the Coal Hill Steakhouse was right next door.

The food was as amazing as the view. I sat at a table right against the window and watched the barges going up and down the river while eating what I would have to say is the PERFECT meal for me. Started off with calamari, and then a Pittsburgh salad (minus the olives). What is a Pittsburgh salad you ask? Well, the menu described it as this: "mixed field greens, grilled chicken, cucumber, tomato, onions, pepperoncini, Kalamata olives, shredded cheese...and French fries." The restaurant also had their walls covered with Steelers memorabilia, including a series of photos taken when they imploded the old Three Rivers Stadium in 2001.

After a very leisurely lunch and a lot of time resting and chatting with my server, I headed to the stadium. The rain had stopped and I am sure that it had delayed a lot of the crowd, luckily for me. The drive and the parking was quick and easy…but the walk in, although not farther than what I would consider normal, was a struggle for me. Again, I took my time…I had no obligations and could do as much or as little as I was able.

The tickets you get are for entry, you can sit wherever you want in the sections they have open. Since Covid was still keeping people distancing, I was able to find a seat not too close to anyone, but still on the field level, about 10 rows back.

I had never seen professional football team training…

but it was similar to the training I watched when my kids played. The theory works in life as well as sports. Break down the important skills and run them over and over until you can run them smoothly, without thought. I was a gymnast growing up and I had a coach that taught me to run my routines over and over. The entire routine, chunks of the routine, and individual runs of the routine. Repeat. And Repeat. Repeat until your body knows every move and what it feels like.

Repeat until you could run through it in your mind and your body would respond with what it felt to do that move. That was what I was watching on the field. To many it would be boring, players broken into small groups doing the same move over and over until it came time to switch to a different skill. After a number of switches, they would all come together and run a few downs of a scrimmage and then break back into small groups.

The best part of the day was watching the kids…all decked out in their Steelers gear, cheering on their favorite players. In between scrimmage sessions, some of the players would come over and wave to their fans.

As the clouds went away and the sun came out it got too hot for me to sit out in the open and I took off for my last spot of the day, and this one was something special.

Randyland…yes that is the name. It is an outdoor art museum created and maintained by artist Randy Gilson himself. The address is 1501 Arch Street, and don't worry…you won't miss it. It is located in what is called the "North Side" and is open most days, even if the hours are not always consistent. It is free but donations are accepted if you enjoyed your visit.

It is filled with the most colorful, eclectic, recycled, materials you can imagine. You would think that it would be overwhelming and over stimulating…but somehow it works. It was a shady respite and a cool place to relax after the football stadium. It made me want to go create something! Randy wasn't there, but I did get to chat with Tom who was running the show that day. He had great stories about Randy and how this project started back in 1995. I talked with other guests there and even the ones who live in Pittsburgh had never been there before. This is a must-see for everyone. If you love art and creating, plan on spending some time there seeking out the hidden gems. Make sure you go to my website to check out the pictures. They will give you a glimpse of the fun folly, but will not do justice to this gem of a spot.

I spent a little over an hour there. I would have liked to spend more time but the sky was getting dark again and I was running very low on energy so back to the hotel I went.

I dropped the car off in the parking lot of the hotel to run across the street to the closest restaurant before the rain started up again. Just as I did I get a text message from the Nation's Weather Service with a tornado and severe thunderstorm warning. The first one of the trip…but not the last.

Day 3: Friday, July 30

My plan was to go back into the city but woke up way too tired to do that. I decided to lay low and work on photos while I had some time. I wrote, relaxed and just enjoyed the freedom of being able to decide what I would do next. I was beginning to like having unstructured days, but I was still frustrated with my health and the slow pace I was moving at, and the fact that it took me so long to recover. I was determined to do as much as I could…but not be upset if I needed a nap to accomplish it.

After relaxing all morning, I decided to hit the road. It was a short drive to Steubenville, Ohio for the Defending the Faith Conference.

Chapter 11
Heaven on Earth

"Surrounded by Your glory
What will my heart feel?
Will I dance for You Jesus
Or in awe of You be still?
Will I stand in Your presence
Or to my knees, will I fall?
Will I sing hallelujah?
Will I be able to speak at all?
I can only imagine"

"I Can Only Imagine"
Recorded by MercyMe

Writer: Bart Millard

Day 3-5: Friday, July 30 to Sunday, August 1

The Franciscan University of Steubenville is a private Catholic university located in Steubenville, Ohio. It overlooks the Ohio River at the point where Ohio, West Virginia and Pennsylvania meet. If you fly in for the conference, you will fly into Pittsburgh as it is about an hour away.

The University of Steubenville was founded in 1946 by the Franciscan Friars of the Third Order Regular and is committed to the integration of faith and reason in all aspects of education. They offer a range of undergraduate and graduate programs in various fields, including theology, philosophy, education, business, and the liberal arts, and are known for their strong emphasis on Catholic teachings and their commitment to academic excellence.

The campus culture is deeply rooted in Catholic traditions, with daily Mass, prayer, and spiritual activities playing a central role in university life and they strive to instill a strong sense of faith and virtue in their students.

The conference I was attending was "Defending the Faith", one of the Adult Summer Conferences hosted annually by the school. The conference aims to deepen the understanding of the Catholic faith for the attendees, equip them with apologetic tools, and inspire them to live and share their faith in the modern world.

This was my 20th year at the conference. It has become a "spiritual booster shot" for me. My mother was able to attend with me several times and one of the 2 years I missed was the year she died. Over the years our group that attends together varied in size, but this year, because of the Covid protocols in place, it was just me, one of my best friends, and her husband.

Another thing different about this year is to keep with the "adventure" theme of my trip, I opted to stay on campus in one of the dorms instead of at a hotel.

The drive in was quick and I spent the time listening to CDs (yes...I still listen to CDs) of past talks from the Conference helping me to shift into the spiritual mode. I wasn't in a hurry, but I hoped to get there in time to check in and drop my stuff in my dorm room before the "Early Bird" Sessions started at 2:00. That is when my first problem became apparent.

I had forgotten how hilly the campus was. Just walking from my car to the building to register had me winded. Luckily there were chairs in the hallway for me to catch my breath. While waiting in line I had my second problem pop up…and this was a big one.

Several of the dorms had been renovated but there were still a few that weren't, which meant no elevators. AND no air-conditioning. Now, when I registered in April, air conditioning wasn't really a concern. Now in late July…it was. After the 3 women in front of me all got placed in a dorm with no elevators, I was ecstatic to learn I was in the dorm with one.

The final problem…parking. There are always many more people than parking spaces and the only one I found was by the main conference area, but a long, hilly walk to the dorm. I solved that problem by making one small trip at a time. Attend a session, grab something from the car and take it to the dorm. It was tedious and often frustrating, but I was determined to conquer my nemesis...the stairs AND it helped that I could take a lot of breaks. The campus is beautiful and luckily there are benches and tables scattered around.

Meals were provided under 2 huge tents. Again, at the top of a hill. After all the years of attending the conference, I took my first shuttle ride. They have shuttles that circle around the campus and the local hotels and they will take you wherever you need to go, whenever you need to get there. They were a lifesaver for me.

The conference starts Friday afternoon with what they call "Early Bird" sessions followed by a travelers' Mass. Then the official kick-off of the conference is Friday night. Saturday starts with Mass and speakers, then after lunch, 2 rounds of small breakout sessions with varying topics.

Saturday evening is the keynote talk by Dr. Scott Hahn followed by the pinnacle of the weekend, a Eucharistic Holy Hour. I can't begin to explain how moving the Holy Hour is. 1000 people, packed in a university gym, on their knees in worship…in song…and sometimes in silence so still you can hear a pin drop.

The Eucharistic procession is a sacred and profound ceremony that transcends the boundaries of time and space. The host, transformed through the sacred act of consecration into the true Body, Blood, Soul, and Divinity of Christ under the appearance of bread, is reverently carried through the room. Up and down the aisles. The room is dark, except for a spotlight shining upon the Monstrance holding the host and being lifted high by the priest. Leading the procession is a server carrying the Cross, followed by 2 servers carrying candles, and another walking backward, facing the priest and swinging a thurible which is a metal container with a lid. It is often intricately decorated and is suspended from chains. Inside the thurible, there is a container to hold lit charcoal, and incense is placed on top of the coals. When the thurible is swung, it produces a fragrant smoke that sanctifies and purifies the people and symbolizes the prayers of the faithful rising to heaven.

It is an extremely moving and powerful night which always leaves me in tears. As a Catholic, we believe that Jesus is truly present in the Eucharist, and so He is there… walking among us. Inviting us to come closer, love deeper, trust more fully. Even though it is a Catholic Conference, there are participants who are not Catholic, and even they are moved by the evening.

In past years, I would often leave the Holy Hour and head to the Portiuncula for prayer. It is a small chapel on the University grounds that is a re-creation of the 13th Century church of the same name rebuilt by St Francis outside of Assisi. That wouldn't be happening this year as I was too tired and there were still a lot of steps to get to my dorm room.

Staying in the dorm certainly added to the road trip experience. No special mattress and soft sheets. No private bathroom. At least I did end up getting a room with an air conditioner.

Meal time is always a favorite of mine…not just because I love food, but because I always try to find new people to sit with. It is so moving to see where people are from and hear the story of how they came to the conference. And you know me, it's ALL about the story.

This year I met a woman from Ohio named Pat, who was at the conference by herself also. It seemed that we found ourselves at the same table at most of the meals. It is always inspiring to hear what others take away from the talks as we compare notes and share insights.

Sunday starts with the closing talks and then finishes with Mass. Followed by lots of hugs and goodbyes and we will see you next year!

After that it is a quick check out of the dorm, the lunch they provide is to go so I grab it and hit the road.

The conference has always had a transformative impact on me. I leave there with a deeper understanding of what the Catholic Church teaches and why. My faith grows stronger and I am challenged to go back and live that faith and share it. This year I left with the overwhelming feeling that God had amazing things in store for me…greater than I could even imagine…if I would just surrender and let Him lead me.

I promised to be open and available for whatever comes my way.

Chapter 12
Build an Ark

"Here I am, Lord
Is it I, Lord?
I have heard you calling in the night
I will go Lord, if You lead me
I will hold Your people in my heart"

"Here I am Lord"
Recorded by Collin Raye

Day 6: Monday, August 2

Monday morning finds me at a hotel outside of Cincinnati, Ohio. The drive from Steubenville was about five hours so I didn't have to be in a hurry. I was just starting to get into the vibe of driving and was starting to really enjoy the scenery. I rigged a camera to my rear-view mirror so that I could take pictures while I was driving…as much for mental reminders as to get photos. Some of them were so I could remember to go back and look up more information about something.

Cardinal Power Plant for instance. I had never taken that route out of Steubenville before and not long after I left, I saw this huge power plant sitting right on the river. In one of the photos, I saw a name. When I looked it up I learned that it was the Cardinal Power Plant and it is located in Brilliant, Ohio. What a name! It has 3 coal-fired units that generate up to 1,230 MW. It is one of the cleanest power plants of its kind in the world. Go figure.

I also got a beautiful shot of Paycor Stadium while driving through Cincinnati. It was previously known as Paul Brown Stadium and is an outdoor football stadium home to the Cincinnati Bengals. It was new to me. When I lived in Indiana the Bengals were the local favorites and they played at Riverfront Stadium.

I was supposed to meet up with some old friends in Cincinnati but that ended up not working out, so I drove a little farther, crossing into Kentucky.

This was the first time that I had the thought that I would let God guide this trip for me.

I had been talking to a friend Melissa for weeks, trying

to figure out a place that we could meet. We ran into issues with places not being open, or that Covid restrictions wouldn't let us visit so we came up with a Plan "E" that ended up being a total blast.

We were looking for a place that was close to my route and not too far away from her and we came up with "The Ark Encounter". I had heard of it but had NO idea what to expect when Mel suggested it.

The Ark Encounter is a biblical theme park and tourist attraction located in Williamstown, Kentucky, about a half hour from Cincinnati. It features a life-sized replica of Noah's Ark, as described in the Bible. Literally. Life. Sized. A 510-foot long, 85-foot wide and 51-foot high boat. In the middle of nowhere.

The ark was constructed using a combination of modern construction techniques and materials while aiming to stay true to the biblical dimensions and descriptions.

If you like museums, you will love this. As you enter the Ark, you will see three levels of stunning exhibits giving you a glimpse into what Noah's life might have been like.

Deck one blew me away with the sheer size of the Ark and showed what the storage situation might have looked like.

Deck two focuses on the pre-flood world, animal concerns (and there were most likely plenty of them), and an exploration of Noah and how God could have prepared him for his monumental task.

Deck three covers what the living quarters for Noah and his family might have been like, flood geology, post-flood events, and a special Museum of the Bible exhibit.

I was impressed by how much science was present in the exhibits, even though the whole point of the park is biblical. It would be enjoyable and thought-provoking even for non-believers.

I felt a connection with Noah with all the planning and preparation I had to do for my trip and it was only 6 weeks. And luckily, I had no animals to worry about.

I was really moved by the thought of Noah…working hard to build this huge vessel. Probably being mocked and ridiculed. I wonder if he ever questioned God. If he asked why me? I can imagine him getting frustrated and thinking to himself "I am not doing this…". Yet, still being obedient to God's call and doing it anyway.

His faith in God's word and answering the call that God gave him would be something that continually came to mind while on my trip. I often feel that I am open to doing God's will…but I am not sure if I could have done what Noah did. I am not sure I can be obedient for what God will call me to do.

Life in the Covid environment where we were continually being pitted against each other was the perfect testing ground. Could you stand up for what you believe… no matter WHAT that was when there were people bashing you from all sides? I had friends with medical conditions that had to be super precautious, get mocked and yelled at. I had friends who were terrified and they were ridiculed. I knew others who looked for questions to be answered and were confronted with hate and threats. It was society at its worst…yet I still believed in my heart that the picture that was presented was not the norm. That when you get away from the media, and the powerful agendas, that your average people are all the same. We want to live a good life, provide for our families, help our neighbors, and support our communities. I wonder if Noah ever felt the same. Some scholars say that it took Noah as long as 75 years to build the Ark. Could you take the harassment for that long? Could you stay true to your calling that long?

I hope that I never have to find out.

We spent hours wandering through the Ark. It was a great place to meet up with Mel as the tour is self-guided so we could take our time and there were plenty of places to sit and rest.

In addition to the ark itself, the Ark Encounter features a petting zoo with live animals, providing a hands-on experience for visitors. There are also beautifully landscaped gardens surrounding the ark, contributing to the overall immersive and beautiful environment.

There were restaurants on site, but we chose to find the closest Mexican place. Mel is one of what I call my "music" friends. We met through a mutual love of Pat Green and his music. We have talked by chat, text, phone, and FB for years, but we have only seen each other in person a few times. She is just one of the many friends like that. If you go through my FB friends list, you will see most of my contacts are musicians, people I met at shows, and people who have become lifelong friends because of the music. I love when I get a chance to catch one of them in person. One great reason to travel!

It was in our conversation that we came up with the term, "Experience based adventure". I decided that I was going to find as many new "experiences" as I could find during the cross-country adventure.

Once lunch was over it was back in my car and off to my old "home" town.

Richmond, Indiana was only two hours away and that would be my first real break.

Chapter 13
Richmond, IN

"You're always 17 in your hometown."

"17"

Recorded by Cross Canadian Ragweed

Writer: Cody Canada

Day 7-10: Tuesday, August 3 to Friday, August 6

I remember how strange it was when we moved to Richmond Indiana.

The area where we lived in Texas was a growing suburb of Houston. It was mostly agricultural when we moved there in 1973. My dad wanted to build a house there because he traveled a lot for his work and it was close to Houston Intercontinental Airport (now George Bush International Airport). The area was booming with new subdivisions and massive growth, with money from the oil industry. It was culturally and ethically rich. I had neighbors from all over the world, mostly upper-middle-class, white-collar workers. I took piano lessons and started playing clarinet in the band. I was in gymnastics and Camp Fire Girls and spent my summers at Camp Winiwaka riding horses, canoeing and swimming in the lake. My mom would drive us to the new Galleria Mall to go skating on the new indoor rink.

I attended Wunderlich Intermediate School and although I don't remember a lot about those days, I know I loved school, especially that school. It was only a year old with lots of windows and outside common areas. The classrooms were open concept with teaching teams. It was a great place to live and a great time to be there.

When I was told that my father got a promotion and we were moving to Indiana all I remember was thinking, "Where the heck is Indiana?" He worked for Belden, a wire and cable manufacturer and they were headquartered there.

To say it was a culture shock is an understatement. Richmond Indiana was a very blue-collar manufacturing town. I transferred to Test Jr High School, which was built in 1922. It was cold and dark looking and I thought the building was a prison the first time I saw it.

Shopping in the area was mostly small local businesses and there were very few restaurants. There was basketball though and my parents, especially my mom, were huge fans.

It was an interesting time for me. I had friends whose fathers were in unions and going on strike. As local factories started to close, I had to watch more than one family have to move when parents got laid off. I was deeply affected when a friend's father lost his job of 15 years.

After leaving Houston, an area that was growing fast, the economic instability of Richmond was tough for me to experience. As my generation grew up and headed to college, most of them did not come back and there was an "exodus" feeling about the town.

That all being said, there were some amazing things about Richmond Indiana too. We had a thriving art culture. At the time, it was believed to have been the smallest community in the US with a professional opera company and symphony orchestra. Richmond also hosted Civic Theater, a community-based program that hosted 6 productions a year with local participation.

I always felt somewhat like an outsider there, though I had a wonderful group of close friends through Junior High and High School. I do have a lot of good memories of my time there and a lot of bad memories too. The same I suppose as any person does when it comes to their hometown. I moved back to Richmond after graduating from college. In 1989, the year after I got married, my parents moved back to Texas, and I moved on to North Carolina.

Over the years I have been back here often. My husband's family is here and I have a few friends who still live in the area. There has always been something sad about coming back, not just in the long-ago memories, but in the town itself. Most of the kids left for college and never came back and so the population was aging dramatically.

For a long time there wasn't much growth in business or population. The schools were failing and there was a rise in drugs and crime. The same story you see in many small towns, especially in the Midwest.

In the last ten years or so, most trips back involved some sort of family emergency, medical crisis, funeral, or responsibility that was challenging and emotional. It was nice that this time the trip was different. I had no commitments, no real plan, and was just going to rest and prepare for the next few weeks of my trip. I was staying at a house that was getting ready to be put on the market for sale, so I had the place to myself. It was quiet. No TV or internet. It was a great place to hide. To prepare and plan. I cooked, and read, and I slept a lot. At least until 3:00 AM Thursday morning.

It had been a while since I had a panic attack but this one hit me out of the blue and it packed a punch. Even with all the walking and hills at the conference I hadn't felt this bad. My meds didn't help. My inhaler didn't help.

Facebook Post
Thursday, August 5, 9:15 AM

I apologize for the long post....

I had a really tough night last night. I woke up at 3 am...that seems to be my bewitching hour and was really struggling. My breathing and heart racing hadn't been that bad in a long time.

I can't really describe what it feels like when I have one of these 'episodes' but it is somewhere between a panic attack and a heart attack. I lay there for hours trying to get back in control and wondering why I was having such a hard time all of a sudden.

Then it hit me what day it was. Aug 5th. I was fairly certain that this was the date my father died, but in my disoriented condition, I really couldn't remember.

I got online trying to find a copy of his obituary, anything that would confirm what I was thinking. No matter where I looked, I couldn't find anything. So then I googled my mom and had no better luck.

It was really disturbing to me, and I felt like so much time has gone by that all proof of their existence was gone. I started to feel a desperation I hadn't felt since having Covid.

After hours of searching, I found an obscure link to an ancestry site that had photos of gravestones and obit information gathered and uploaded by volunteers. I want to thank Joseph Cahill and Rusty Weber. I don't know them but I owe my peace of mind to them.

I finally fell back to sleep at about 5:30. I could see the sun was just getting ready to come up on a new day.

My father died on this day 22 years ago from colon cancer. We were lucky though, when he was diagnosed the doctor told us he had six months to live, but we had him for almost a year and a half. He spent that time fighting the cancer with chemo until the fight just got too hard and the chemo was destroying not only the cancer but his body and his spirit.

He died about two weeks after he stopped chemo treatments.

I suppose this day is particularly hard because I am currently in Richmond Indiana which is where we moved to when we left Texas. I went to high school and college here and there are so many memories of my dad. I think I'll spend the day driving around trying to remember as much as I can.

In the meantime, in memory of my dad, please hug your loved ones, young and old. Tell them what they mean to you. And spent today making a #epicMemory.

I had thrown around the idea of staying in Richmond until Saturday, but I was able to get a hold of a high school friend who was going to meet me for dinner in Indianapolis Friday night, so I stopped by Pizza King (the area favorite pizza place) and picked up pizza to share with my husband's niece and her family…did some laundry and repacked the car.

Facebook Post
Thursday, August 5, 4:04 PM

Week one overview:

Well, week one is in the books...here are a few things I have learned:

1. I love to drive! The is something powerful about hopping in the car and taking off. Witnessing the

changing beauty of the landscape.

2. No matter what social media and the news say... people are kind and wonderful. At least most of them. I have met so many wonderful people... had so many wonderful conversations. Everyone is happy to be out...happy to be enjoying life... and more than willing to do whatever they can to make others comfortable. Places where there were mandatory masks (the Incline in Pittsburgh) people were gracious. There were always people holding doors, offering to take a photo for me, saying hello and SMILING!

3. I miss having younger children around. They have been such a blessing to talk to and to watch. I yearn for their innocence and pure joy.

4. There is so much to see! AND so much amazing food! I am going to come home weighing 500 pounds.

5. Everyone is looking for workers. I saw a sign that Arby's was offering a $500 signing bonus if you came to work there. Luckily, most of what I have seen is people who are completely understanding about the understaffing and the ragged employees. They are doing their best and are handling it well. (Please return the favor and be patient and tip well to those people who are working so hard.)

6. I am very happy with how well I am physically handling this trip so far. Except for the episode this morning, I have been feeling great. I have been pushing myself to walk and spending time every day to start doing some light exercises. I

don't get tired as easy and my blood O2 doesn't drop like it has. The heat and humidity still zap me and my recovery is slower than I would like but I am sure that I can tackle the next 4 1/2 weeks. I may be panting and out of breath but I will do it!

7. Speaking of recovery...I am not getting as much done daily as I hoped, please be patient with updates. I am hoping to get into a routine soon ☺

Thank you to everyone who has supported me on this trip...especially my

#epicTrip Sponsors:

Murray Automotive

Sharvette Mitchell & Mitchell Productions, LLC

Cultivating Sales

and

KWE Publishing, Writing, Coaching, Storytelling

It is never too late to join in the fun...I have business sponsorships available or you can become a #epic Road Warrior by contributing via Venmo or Paypal. Every $ is greatly appreciated and if you give $50 or more you will receive a signed copy of the book of the trip.

Day 10: Friday, August 6

I woke up much more stable than the day before. The sun was shining and I was excited to get moving. I was in no hurry to get to Indianapolis so I did a memory drive around Richmond. The house I lived in...my Dad's green thumb touches were gone and so was the big rock that had been in the front yard, but the house was still the same.

Places I used to work, the local hangouts, my church, the high school, and the last stop…Test Junior High. I got out of my car to take a few pictures. It's funny how it doesn't seem quite as much like a prison as it did the very first time I saw it.

When I got back in the car I programmed my GPS for Indy and checked my messages and email before taking off.

My life shifted dramatically when I opened that first email.

Chapter 14
Back Story

"Oh I don't believe in accidents
Miracles, they don't just happen by chance
As long as my God holds the world in His hands,
I know that there's no such thing as unplanned"

"Unplanned"
Recorded by Matthew West

Writers: Matthew West and Andrew Pruis

It was June 1983. I had graduated and was getting ready to head for college. The world was my oyster. I spent days working and nights hanging out with my boyfriend and my friends. I was young, I was in love. And I soon found out that I was pregnant.

At the time, it actually didn't pose a huge problem for me. I was in love with my boyfriend and marriage had been discussed. The question was timing…I had always been leaning towards after I graduated college, but with this new situation I just stepped into planning my new family. I went from reading "How to prepare for college", to "How to prepare for your baby". "Decorating a dorm room" was replaced by "Decorating a nursery".

Until things changed. I don't remember exactly what it was that changed everything. I don't know exactly when it happened. I know it started with an appointment that was scheduled for an abortion that I didn't go to.

I know it went from there to one night after dinner my boyfriend's family showed up at my house without warning. They were there to ask my parents what we were going to do about my problem. The problem at that point was that my parents didn't know. I hadn't told them. I wasn't that far along…I wanted to tell them I was getting married before I told them I was pregnant. I remember it became obvious that marriage was no longer an option. I had no control over where this meeting was headed and the last thing I remember running upstairs and proceeding to throw up my dinner.

I have to give my parents credit. They were wonderful. Even in the shock of the moment, they stood up for me. After my boyfriend's family left, I heard my parents downstairs talking. I couldn't move. I was caught up in a massive amount of fear and shame. And uncertainty. Not only did I have to face a conversation I wasn't prepared to have, but now the wonderful life I was planning was gone.

When my mom came upstairs she took my hand and put me to bed and said we would talk in the morning. I don't remember much of that conversation. I do remember her one request. That no matter what I decided to do, I would at least attend the first semester of college. I promised her that I would, though I had no idea what would happen after that.

It was strange preparing for college and knowing that I wasn't going to be staying there. We made the decision that I would attend my first semester at Purdue but when we left for winter break I would move to Texas. My Godfather and his family live there and I would be staying with them until the baby came.

I had a very close family friend who suggested an agency there and they had a wonderful reputation of supporting unwed mothers with maternity care and helping them as they made important decisions about their lives and the lives of their babies. I made the decision for adoption immediately. Being adopted myself, I wanted my baby to have a loving, stable family and the best chance possible for a good life. At 18 years old I knew that wasn't something I would be able to give to him or her. I had seen the heartbreak of couples who were unable to conceive and knew that my child could be the answer to their prayers. I never wavered in my decision, never second-guessed it. I felt that this precious life that I had been given to watch over and protect was special, and was going to do great things and he/she needed me to take care of them the short time I had him.

Adoption policies had changed since I was born. My adoption was "closed" meaning there was no contact between my birth family and myself and any information about either of us was sealed unless both parties agreed to having it shared. I have little more than the very basic information about my birth parents. The thing I liked most about the agency I used was that I could choose the parents that would adopt my child. We could have as much contact as all the parties were comfortable with.

Life as a college freshman being pregnant while trying to keep it a secret was an interesting endeavor. Only my closest high school friends knew and it was just easier not to talk about it. At Purdue, there was only one person who officially knew, I was a little sister for a fraternity on campus and one of the pledges that lived there guessed about my situation after watching me dodge drinks and parties. He became quite a help to me the few months I was there.

The semester ended and I was off to Texas.

It was there that I started writing. Journaling for me. Things were so new and happening so fast that I wanted to write it all down so I wouldn't forget. And letters. Lots of letters to Thumper. That is what I started calling the baby. He was a mover and always wanted to make his presence known, so it fit. I wasn't sure that I would ever send the letters to Thumper, but they served as a kind of therapy for me. A chance to put into words everything that I wanted to give him.

My love. My desire for the best things in life for him.

My hope that he would grow up to love and be loved. My complete belief that he was created for a reason and that I was chosen to carry him for a reason and that there were great things in store for him.

Thursday, February 9th, 1984 I gave birth to a perfect, tiny baby boy.

Three days later I got to hold him for the first, and last time.

Chapter 15

The Dream I

Didn't Know I Had

**Jmdt1984 please review your message
from another member of Adopted.com:**

 Adopted.com Support
To Jmdt1984
Aug 6 at 10:34 AM

Dear **Jmdt1984**,

You have the following message from another member regarding your
search:

> I think I know your son. The...

Viewing and replying to any message is FREE OF CHARGE.
Simply log in to view the entire message:

CLICK HERE TO LOG IN INSTANTLY

As always, we wish you the best of luck with your search!
Adopted.com

Reminder:
*You registered with Adopted.com on Apr 27, 2017 while searching
for your child.*

"I'm yours"

"I'm Yours"
Recorded by Jason Mraz

Writers: Joey Hyde and Jason Dyba

Day 10: Friday, August 6

The email was from a website called "Adopted.com", a branch of Ancestory.com that catered to adoption situations.

When I clicked on the message it read,

"I think I know your son. The details match exactly. Please contact me."

In 2017, I received a random message on Facebook. It was from the daughter the birth father had after we were together. She said she knew that her father and I had a child together and she was looking to find any information she could about him. She knew what an emotional situation this was and understood if I wasn't willing to help her, but she was trying anything she could.

After the initial shock, I reached out to her and explained that everything I had concerning the baby, I had given her father years ago, but I would see if the adoption agency had any new letters or pictures that I could share. When I started searching, I realized that the adoption agency no longer existed, and I was at a total loss as to where to check next.

Then I stumbled upon the website, "adopted.com." About that time my health issues were kicking into high gear, and I thought maybe it would be a good idea if I could find some information on my birth parents. I didn't find anything.

Then I wondered if I should search for him.

DISCLAIMER: This is going to come off very strange, but going forward for this story I will continue calling my baby "Thumper". That is what I called him for the 9 months that I carried him. I never wanted to name him because I wanted his adoptive family to give him a special name that would mean something to him and his new family.

I remember being nervous about looking for information on Thumper. He had always been in a protected area of my heart where I let no one in. Having someone ask about him broke the lock on that door but I was terrified to open it. It had been so long. I hadn't gotten any information on him in years. I was sure that I didn't matter in the scheme of things, and he didn't need to be bothered by me. But I had to know. Just to check. I entered the information they asked for and there were no connections. I was surprised at how disappointed I was.

I don't know how many times I read those words. "I think I know your son". At the bottom of the email, it said "Reminder: You registered with Adopted.com on April 27th, 2017 while searching for your child".

There was never any question that I would respond but I was sure that it wouldn't be a match. I looked for him 1561 days before. I was sure it was way too late. I wanted to be respectful of the person reaching out to me, so I clicked on the message which took me to the website and I responded. And they responded, asking what I had named the baby and I explained about calling him Thumper. And they responded. And I responded.

I cannot begin to tell you how strange that conversation was for me. Trying to walk a thin line, with them asking a question and then responding and adding a question of my own. Trying to narrow down the similarities in our answers, while not allowing myself to have any hope that this could be true.

Meanwhile, I am driving to Indianapolis and having to pull over every few minutes and respond to the next message I received. After a few exchanges, I was asked if I played basketball in college. The answer was no...but I was afraid to type it. I knew that this wasn't going to be a match but I had let myself get my hopes up. I knew it was too good to be true.

I had dinner plans that evening with my high school friend and had to pause the conversation but said I would respond later that evening. I asked who it was that I was talking to and she said that she was a family friend of Thumper's and had been helping him look for me. He was at work and she was relaying my messages to him.

I figured that dinner would be tough and that I would be distracted by what was transpiring but to my surprise, I wasn't. I was certain that nothing would come of this conversation and ended up having a long, wonderful dinner.

After lots of stories and memories and laughs we said goodbye, I found a hotel and checked in. I was not in a big hurry because I was sure the conversation would be over soon. When I reached back out we exchanged more messages. Back and forth. We ended up switching to texting each other directly because of the tediousness of going through the adopted.com website and I wanted to send her a picture of me from high school. Thumper was sure he would recognize me if I was his birth mother based on a picture of me he had when he was younger but had since lost.

The picture I sent didn't help so she sent me a baby picture of him.

You know in the movies when they want to add dramatic effect, they slow the motion down so it passes screen by screen as if time is stopping? Well, that happens in real life too. The moment I saw that picture, time stopped. My heart stopped. I gasped and then I burst into tears. You see that picture she sent was the exact same picture that I had tucked away in a box in my office at home. There was no question. He was my son.

I asked her to give Thumper my number and if he felt comfortable in reaching out to me I would answer any questions he had and would tell him everything I could. I needed to step away. I needed to think. This was not something I was prepared for. I never...never...EVER imagined this would happen.

I texted my husband and told him what was going on and said that I was heading to the pool to swim laps...shift my focus. Get my head straight.

The hotel pool was closed.

So, I sat in a pool chair and cried.

Thursday, August 5, 9:15 AM
"Hi Jean..."

His first text. I read it. And read it again. And again. Then I respond.

"...I too have thought of you and prayed that you were safe and loved as much as I loved you. I was adopted as a baby and never did I question that my adoptive parents were my 'parents' and hoped you felt that way too.

Funny, I have spent years planning what I would say

to you and now it is all stuck in my heart and won't come out. I am truly at a loss for words and someday I hope you know me well enough to know that NEVER happens."

I have so many questions. He has so many questions. Back and forth.

Who am I?

Who are you?

It is strange getting to know someone. To learn about someone Over the years I wondered so many things and I wanted to get all those answers. First though, I needed to step away for a moment. This was all such a shock. I needed some time to process and I had an early start the next day.

Chapter 16

The Most Famous Words In Motor Sports...

"Start the car, we gotta move
This ain't no living, this ain't no groove
It's been a long hard road
Come on baby (ooh baby)
Let's drive it home
Start the car"

"Start the Car"
Recorded by Travis Tritt

Writer: Jude Anthony Cole

Day 11: Saturday, August 7

In 2018 I decided to start a podcast. It had nothing to do with my business, it was just a passion project. Shortly after that decision, I became the Managing Director for our local eWomenNetwork chapter and that plan got put on hold.

I officially launched the "What's Your Story" podcast in April of 2019. It was my vision to invite people to tell their stories. Everyday people like you and me. I have always loved meeting new people and finding out what their stories are. I also feel that it is important to listen to others' stories because that helps connect us and allows us to see the world through their eyes. My health interfered with everything in 2020 and I didn't get any episodes out at all, but with the start of 2021 I was motivated to get going again and to build consistency. What a wonderful time to take a road trip and have access to new people to interview!

Today was my first #epicRoadTrip interview. I met up with Pam, an Indianapolis-based artist and an acquaintance from high school. I had been following her on Facebook and loved to watch her create. She had a very unique style that was fun and whimsical…but could also be very dramatic. Her house/studio was filled with all sorts of color and art of hers and others. We had a wonderful conversation about art and history and Richmond, Indiana. I would have loved to stay longer but there were miles I needed to make and I had one more stop before leaving Indy.

"Gentlemen, start your engines…" It is believed that, as president of the Indianapolis Motor Speedway, Wilbur Shaw gave that first command before the 1946 Indianapolis

500 race. As women started to join the competition it was changed to "Ladies and Gentlemen" but now it is pretty standard to hear "Drivers start your engines". Just one of the things I read at the Indianapolis Motor Speedway Museum.

There are two things I had to learn about quickly when I moved to Indiana. The first: basketball, and the second: racing at Indianapolis Motor Speedway. The speedway has a passionate fan base, and the Indy 500 attracts spectators from around the world.

The month of May is particularly significant, with a series of events leading up to the Indy 500 race, including practice sessions, qualifying, and the famous Carb Day. Of course, everyone has a favorite driver.

I have never seen a race in Indy. Once, many, MANY years ago I went to the time trials but I was looking forward to checking it out when there weren't 200,000 other people there.

I am a geek for museums and although I know nothing about cars, I was fascinated by seeing how the car designs changed over the years, learning about the racers and the racing "families", even the exhibit on tires was cool. The museum has over 300 vehicles and of course the famed "Borg-Warner Trophy". This sterling silver trophy has been the symbol of victory at the IMS since its unveiling in 1936. Each year a silver likeness of the winner is added to the trophy, and the winner is presented a smaller replica of the award. There are 101 faces on the trophy and the last driver to be added to the ORIGINAL trophy was Bobby Rahal in 1986. Which filled up all the squares. They then made a new base for the trophy but that was filled in 2003.

In 2004 a new base was added that will not be filled until 2034. I wonder what will happen after that? And by the way…yes…the faces are a bit creepy looking.

After wandering through the museum, I bought a ticket for the "View from the Top" Tour. Which included a stop for photos at the Victory Podium and a tour of the 153-foot tall Pagoda which gives you a spectacular view of the Speedway and the downtown skyline. The tour was worth every penny as the tour guides were knowledgeable and fun, and willing to take lots of pictures for you.

My favorite part of the day though, was after the tour was over. I left the museum and headed out to turn two where there was a little observation hill. BMW was testing cars on the road course track so I sat and watched them. It was a beautiful day. The sun was shining. And I found my son. I spent a lot of time re-reading the texts. I wasn't even sure any of this was real. I knew the chances were slim that anything would come of it. I was determined not to get my hopes up.

All that being said, there were new feelings I had as I just sat and watched. Ones I hadn't had in a while.

Peace.

Contentment.

Hope.

I wasn't sure how long it would last but I knew I would enjoy every day I could have it.

Chapter 17

Boiler Up

"There's a spot on earth a man can go
To find himself and free his soul
A place somewhere between hell and heaven
Where no one hurts and all's forgiven
A door that leads to light and grace
But the keys are in the darkest place
Though it feels like I've been there before
Though I don't know what I'm looking for
And I'm trying to find it"

"Trying to Find It"
Recorded by Pat Green

Writers: Jeffrey Steele and Tom Hambridge

Day 11: Saturday, August 7

Still moving. Just a short seventy miles or so north from Indianapolis and I hit West Lafayette, Indiana. Home of Purdue University.

Purdue University was founded in 1869 under the Morrill Land-Grant Act, which provided federal lands for the establishment of colleges focusing on agriculture and the mechanical arts. It is known for its strong academic programs, particularly in engineering, technology, agriculture, business, and the sciences. It has consistently ranked among the top public universities in the United States. The College of Engineering, in particular, is highly regarded, and the university has been a pioneer in aerospace engineering and astronautics.

My favorite Purdue fact? The University is called the "cradle of astronauts" as twenty-seven astronauts graduated from Purdue including:

Gus Grissom, the second American in space.

Neil Armstrong, the first person on the moon.

Gene Cernan, the most recent person on the moon.

Loren Shriver, who commanded the Space Shuttle to a record altitude of 380 miles above the earth.

Janice Voss, who set a record for female astronauts with five spaceflights.

David Wolf, the first person to vote from space.

Jerry Ross, who set records with seven missions and nine spacewalks.

Drew Feustel, third all-time in hours spent spacewalking.

Beth Moses, the first female commercial astronaut.

In fact, nearly a third of all U.S. space flights have included a Purdue grad, and eleven missions have included multiple Purdue grads.

Of course, I was never anywhere near the Aeronautical Engineering classrooms. I was in the School of Consumer and Family Sciences with a major in Retail Management.

When I left Purdue after that first semester I toyed with the idea of transferring to a school in Texas. I decided against that and after Thumper was born I moved back to Richmond and did an off-campus design practicum until Summer school started and then headed back to West Lafayette.

When I moved back to campus and back into a dorm Summer of 1984, I was still very emotional and not really wanting to have any close contact with others so I got a single room, which was perfect, and only available during the summer. The one thing that was missing? When I was there before, I was pregnant and I always had Thumper with me and found myself talking to him a lot.

Now that I was back, I missed just having him with me and decided I needed a pet. The list of pets allowed in a dorm room is very, very small. In fact, basically you can only have a fish. Of course, I had to do things my way and when I went to the store to get a fish, I came home with a piranha. And named him George.

At that point I was mainly focused on getting my degree and moving on. I loved West Lafayette and all that the campus had to offer, but I was past the point of partying on the weekends. My friend had left the Frat house and I had no more connections there and I just didn't seem to have the temperament or desire to start and nurture any new friendships. My only goal was to graduate with as little debt as possible. So I worked a lot. Often two or three jobs at a time. Anything to fill the days and the nights. It took me two years and a lot of tears before I felt ready to venture out again. And I did, just in time to connect with my now husband.

I had moved into a new apartment and bought some furniture and needed help getting it unloaded and set up. I reached out to a guy that I knew with a promise of a payment in beer and he said he'd come over and would bring a few of his roommates to help.

One of those roommates was Dan. We went to the same high school but he graduated two years before me. He was a baseball player and I'd had a crush on him for years. It was a huge surprise when he walked in the door. Dan and I sat on the floor (I couldn't afford a couch yet) and while the other guys moved and set up my furniture Dan and I talked about Richmond, Indiana and all the people we knew. It seems amazing now, 37 years later, but we have been together since that night.

For the next eighteen months, my emotional connection to Purdue shifted. All the memories of Thumper and what happened got put away. Buried deep in my heart with the door locked shut. I would occasionally get letters from the adoptive mother, a picture every so often but as the years went by they were fewer and fewer.

I did send him a letter. Right before I got married. It was filled with information about me and school and work and wedding plans...I hated it. I sounded like some tour guide leading people through an old abandoned building. Pointing out "this" and "that". I couldn't tell him what I really wanted to tell him. I couldn't tell him how much I loved him and how much of me was empty. I couldn't tell him how I fought for him, and how for 9 months I did nothing but live for him. I couldn't tell him that I would do anything for him to be happy and healthy and loved. I couldn't tell him that I knew he was special, that there was a reason that he was born and that he had many beautiful gifts to give the world. I couldn't write any of that.

So I mailed the letter as it was…with all of the rest attached in a prayer.

Everything came crashing in on me when I pulled onto campus. All the emotions and all the memories. I had only been back to campus two times since I graduated and as I drove around, I was overwhelmed by how different everything was. I got lost several times, even with my GPS. I couldn't find my old dorms; I couldn't find my favorite classrooms. I couldn't find my old apartment where I would sit and watch the planes take off from the tiny airport on campus. I couldn't find anything. It wasn't that I expected campus to be exactly like it was when I left it, but everything seemed so foreign. So distant.

At some point in time, I slipped into a full-blown panic attack. Looking back, I think I was trying to find something that would trigger a memory, a connection, a feeling of Thumper from back then, a feeling of who I was back then.

He was always a baby in my mind and now talking to a 37-year-old version of that baby threw me way off kilter. I can't even explain how unreal it all felt, I felt like it may have been all my imagination.

As I stopped for a late lunch there were more texts with Thumper. We talked about our first jobs, my business and what this road trip was for. We talked about family. I asked him if he was angry about being adopted. He asked me if I thought about him on his birthdays.

I wanted to make sure he understood.

Text Message

"...please believe one thing...it was never ever a situation that I didn't want you. I knew, I believed firmly, totally, that it was best for you. I never wavered. I never questioned it. I was sad, and I always wondered where you were and what you were doing and how you were feeling..."

One thing I found amazing was that Thumper said for years he had thought about trying to find me but was worried about being selfish for reaching out to me, he didn't want to disrupt my life. Little did he know that I had given up hope of connecting with him years before. I still haven't quite figured out why the desire to know him was so much stronger than my desire to know MY birth parents.

I was finally able to locate the house that Dan lived in when we met...and Happy Hollow Park, where we had our first "date". That would have to be enough. I was emotionally drained and still had a few hours drive to Chicago where I was staying with some family friends. I expected lots of traffic and lots to think about.

Chapter 18

Chicago and St. Michael the Arc Angel

"On my way to wonderful I found you,
It feels so good to be around you"

"On My Way to Wonderful"
Recorded by Wade Bowen

Writers: Seth James and Wade Bowen

Day 11: Saturday, August 7

At some point I stopped for gas. Thumper and I were still texting back and forth every so often. He told me about having a photo of me that his adopted mother had given him, and how much we looked alike.

I told him that I had to return a call from my youngest. I had left him a message earlier and he just tried to get back to me.

Text Message

"Now wish me luck. I'm actually calling my youngest son to tell him about you. Again, I never thought this would happen, so I never talked about you. You were always my gift that I held on tight to myself. This might take a minute so I'm not going to answer you back right away"

Thumper seemed surprised that they didn't know.

"My husband knows. A few friends from high school that obviously knew. You were mine. I did not want to share my memories of you."

"Thank you for being so understanding. There's certainly no textbook on how to get through this situation".

Chicago has always been a favorite place of mine. Both my parents were from there and we had lots of family and friends that are even now still in the area. My love for travel was born from my mother loading my brother and I into the car and driving from Houston to Chicago. Since my dad traveled a lot for work, she was often alone. From her I also got a love and a commitment to family. My memories are filled with Thanksgivings and Christmases and even vacations with cousins and aunts and uncles. My mother's parents lived on the Southside of Chicago and I remember summers at their house, trips to Lincoln Park and the Zoo, the History Museum and Shedd Aquarium.

While in Chicago I stayed with some family friends. People who had known me all my life. They were great friends of my parents and it was comforting to spend time with them hearing stories of how wonderful I was when I was younger…and how horrible my brother was!

For the first time in a long time, I felt a connection to my parents. I lost them both so long ago, my dad in 1997 and my mother in 2002. I have so many wonderful memories, but time has stolen the feeling of them being there.

There are so many things I would have loved to do while in Chicago, but my stop there was really focused on one thing…getting a chance to see my Aunt Connie.

She was the youngest in my father's family and someone I was very close to. She helped me a lot during the final years of my mom's life and was always my go-to when I had questions or just needed to vent. Her strength and support got me through some of my toughest days.

Her husband had died a few years before and when I went to Chicago for his funeral, I noticed that she was starting to repeat stories and to not remember things that were just said. I knew that this might be the last time I got to see her and even though she had no idea who I was, it was important for me just to spend some time with her.

If you have a friend or family member dealing with memory loss and dementia, I applaud you and I will pray for you. It is a heartbreaking, painful and scary place to be.

At the same time, there is a true simplicity there. My aunt looked the same, had the same beautiful smile, yet it was obvious that she had no idea what we were talking about.

My cousin made sure to include her in the conversation and the times she spoke it was usually a sort of gibberish… but she did participate and that was a beautiful thing. Our visit was short as she tired easily and it was time for her after lunch drive. Part of her routine that brought her comfort and peace in a world that she didn't recognize.

I knew that it was most likely the last time I would see her, but what really made me sad was that I wasn't able to share what was happening with Thumper and my reaction to the situation. Connie had spent her life in social work, specializing in helping children. I know she would have a unique perspective and be the perfect person to keep me in check. You see, that was a concern for me from the very beginning. These stories often don't have a happy ending. Feelings of guilt, abandonment, and trauma are frequent. I may have felt that I knew Thumper after 9 months of carrying him, but I didn't know the 37-year-old man he became. Or know what his agenda was. I even said to him:

Text Message

"This had been an incredible situation, one I thought never would happen. But when it comes down to it, we are strangers. I know of and have worked with enough post-adoptive situations to know there are 101 ways that this could blow up in both of our faces."

From the very first text, I promised Thumper that I would answer any questions he had as best I could, and I promised myself that I would not lose control. Our connection was a miracle, but that miracle wasn't guaranteed to be a positive thing. I asked him if he was angry about being adopted.

Text Message

"I never ever, ever imagined this would happen, but I wonder, were you ever angry about being adopted? That is an honest question, you can answer it honestly. I always wondered if I was weird because I never felt like I didn't know who I was because I was adopted and I feel like people kept expecting me to feel that way."

So often that is the response I get from other adoptees. Anger at being left, feeling abandoned. A desire for revenge. It happens. But that wasn't what I was getting in our conversations. Thumper seemed truly happy that we connected, seemed excited about being able to build some kind of relationship between us, and our families. He even voiced concern over all my health issues saying that I needed to take care of myself because we only just met, he didn't want something to happen to me. In fact, he said everything that a birth mother would want to hear.

So much so that part of me was a bit concerned about my ability to stay rational and in control. I did reach out to a friend who I knew would be totally supportive in this situation, but who was also wary enough to be protective and would be able and willing to keep me in check if my emotions took over. She promised to wheel me in if I started going out of control.

I was also worried about how this was affecting Thumper. Was he really prepared to know me? Learn about his birth father? I had never really thought about MY birth parents, but what if I was a disappointment to Thumper? What if talking to me was making his life harder? I told him:

Text Message

If things get hard...even with me, I beg you to tell me and we can back off. I will not come this far to put you in jeopardy"..."and know that there are no questions...no problems that we can't work out. No judgment ever. This has been a miracle to me. And remember, I fiercely protected you once...against all odds. I will do it again if need be...Whether we have one conversation or 10, at least I know you exist."

Day 12: Sunday, August 8

Sunday Mass is very important to me. In fact, if time permitted, I would go every day. It is so much a part of who I am and what I need to survive. Where I am going to attend Mass is always a great project. Sometimes I have no choice...there is one church with one Mass time... but here in Chicago the choices were endless. Which is closest? What Mass times were available? Sometimes those questions make the decision easy. Sometimes there is just one that jumps out to me. THAT is how I ended up at St. Michael the Archangel Parish for Mass that morning.

You might think I am crazy, and I promise, in many ways I am, but I have always felt that St. Michael was watching over me. I know that he has been there for me more than once. I prayed that God would allow him to stay with me during this trip. I admit, I was afraid. Not afraid for my physical self, but I knew that finding Thumper was unlocking doors that I had thought were closed for good.

I wasn't sure where this was going to go…I wasn't sure that I trusted myself to stay impartial…I knew that I had started tearing down walls that I had built years ago. And as Thumper started asking about his birth father, I knew that some very old painful wounds were about to be opened. I think there were people at Mass who were worried about me because I sat in the pew for quite a while when Mass was over. Just sobbing.

Still Day 12: Sunday, August 8

This #epicRoadtrip was supposed to be about my business. The business of DREAMING. Turns out I wasn't getting much work done. There was ONE thing that had to get completed. I was one of a group of writers putting together an anthology book. There was a lot of emailing, proofing, and editing that had to be done. As well as working on my agenda for the next few days. Sunday night, after an amazing dinner, I sat at my friend's table and worked.

My work…edited and submitted.

Emails sent.

Research done.

More conversations with Thumper.

Family. Struggles. Hopes. Sports. Work. The past and the future. Books we love. Favorite movies. Things we love. And whether or not pineapple belongs on pizza.

Text Message

"I talked to you a lot over the years…you just weren't with me. Mostly (I said) that I loved you. That I knew you had greatness and that you were saved for something

special. Sometimes as simple as goodnight, I hope you had a wonderful day.

For years I made chocolate cupcakes on your birthday.

As my kids came and grew up and needed more attention there weren't as many direct thoughts specifically, but I would catch myself wondering if you played basketball or if you love to swim. What classes you liked, if you had a girlfriend. If you wondered about me."

"I feel better because I know you are here. And to be totally honest and transparent, in my mind you were always just mine. That is selfish and unreasonable but that is the way it was. That's one reason I never talked about you."

He was caring, funny, and sarcastic. And so much like me it was scary. Also scary, how much we had in common. So many strange connections. I couldn't help but feel that this was meant to happen. We were meant to be connected; it just took waiting until the time was right.

It had been a long time since I thought that much about who I am. Who I want to be. What I love and why. He made me laugh…and I told him that he was the best "babysitter" for keeping me so entertained. Getting to know him was exhilarating and hopeful.

I really believe that music is a window to your soul…a piece of who you are. I ended the conversation that night asking him for a list of his top ten favorite songs. Then I wondered if I could narrow MY list down to ten.

Day 13: Monday, August 9

One last stop before I head out of town. Queen of Heaven Cemetery. My parents are buried here, and so are my father's parents.

Facebook Post
Monday, August 9, 2:05 PM

Drying my tears and getting on with my Epic Road Trip 2021...Mom would be proud...

Authenticity they say. It has been my mantra since I started planning this trip. Well, here's authentic for you...sitting in the rain mud under my fingernails, covered in dirt.

I know my parents aren't here, but yet there's something comforting about coming back.

The first leg of this trip has turned out to be very emotional. Some amazing things have happened, but yet still very emotional. Somehow sitting here makes things a little better.

Sometimes you just need your mom...and dad.

#epicisnotalwayeasy

#ichoseepic

#epiclivingwithjean

#queenofheavencemetery #imissmymom

I cleaned the dirt and grass off of their stones and just sat there.

I am not sure how long I sat in the rain.

Long enough to tell them how Thumper had found me.

Long enough to tell them how it felt when he texted "I'm your son".

Long enough to tell them that he had asked if he could call me so we could talk but I was scared and so I said I wasn't ready.

As I left Chicago and headed north to Wisconsin, I had this terrible feeling that it was all about to unravel. I was terrified that something would happen to my phone and all these amazing messages would be lost so I did what any smart businesswoman would do. I took a screenshot of each one and sent them to be backed up.

Chapter 19

Wisconsin: Cool People Doing Cool Things

"Oh am I
Am I, am I, crazy enough
Is this life what I've always dreamed of
Oh it raises all kinds of questions
Yeah, it stirs my pot of thoughts
Am I, am I crazy enough"

"Crazy Enough"
Recorded by Wade Bowen

Writers: Wade Bowen and Jeremy Nathan Spillman

Day 13: Monday, August 9
Mukwonago, Wisconsin

I just love the sound of it. Especially since I am stopping here to meet with some of my favorite people. Melissa Blair and her daughter Stephanie are the foundation of Cultivating Sales, a company that has built the ultimate marketing, sales, automation, CRM platform out there. They not only revolutionized every aspect of my business; they are also a sponsor for my road trip.

When I check in to my hotel there is a Tornado watch popping up on the TV screen in the lobby. Little did I know that that would be a recurring theme the next few days.

I get settled in my room and get down to work. I will be interviewing Melissa and Stephanie at their office tomorrow and Melissa and I are meeting for dinner to go over our plans and to catch up. She has been a huge asset to me the last few months. When I took the Dream Manager certification, I had no idea how I would implement the program. I wanted my food company customers, mostly mothers, teachers, bank tellers, to have access to this program because I knew that they definitely needed to remember how to Dream. It was Melissa and Stephanie who guided me through the process of building the systems I would need to not only build a Dream Manager program but to automate my food company to be able to streamline my processes and serve my customers better. I was looking forward to spending time with them.

I also had a LONG list of work to catch up on. This trip was looking less and less about work, but I did have some priority things that needed to happen.

This is where I woke up this morning...not sure how to pronounce it but I love it.

Excited about meeting up with Melissa Blair from #epicTrip Sponsor Cultivating Sales. We will be talking about systems, automation and follow-up. Whether your business is big or small these are things you need to think about.

Then I'm spending the afternoon locked in my hotel room, posting all the pictures and stories from the last couple days. I'm sorry that I have been a little lax and doing that, but this has turned into the most exhilarating, wonderful, trip that I could've ever imagined.

But first, I need to get out and walk

I had a blast with Melissa and Stephanie. I love getting to work with strong, smart women, who have a vision and are willing to do what it takes to make it work. We had a lot of laughs. My favorite line of the day was when Melissa said that she gets to work with "cool people...doing cool things". Yeah...That includes me! I have been with them for a long time, long before I even needed all their services because I saw their vision and I knew how it would change my business. AND it has.

In the years since then, they have made it even better and I depend on them even more.

Facebook Post
Tuesday, August 10, 8:35 PM

Would someone tell me why I didn't stop by Three Crosses Distilling Company and pick up a bottle of vodka before I left town? I could use it about now.

When I checked in yesterday there was a tornado watch...Last night a storm blew the power out in our hotel. And today there's another crazy storm rolling in...

One of the things I love about traveling is all the people that you meet. I was re-organizing the car…trying to get everything done before the rain started and ended up talking to a lady that was parked next to me. She worked for an insurance company and traveled around doing damage estimates for property after natural disasters. We shared travel tips and travel stories right up until the rain started. Then I ran for cover and hung out with a group of guys who worked for the power company and traveled around the state repairing downed lines while we ate vending machine snacks and watched the lightning.

Facebook Post
Tuesday, August 10, 8:35 PM

The wicked storm that blew up brought some nasty weather and a cosmic black hole that sucked the life out of everything I touched today. But that's ok, tomorrow's another day! Hoping I will announce a new podcast episode if I can get everything working again!

Now maybe a few hours' sleep until we are off again.

#baddayscanstillbeepic
#ichoseepic
#epiclivingwithjean
#howamistillawake

Chapter 20

Minnesota: Tornado Warning

> ⚠ EMERGENCY ALERTS
>
> **Emergency Alert**
> National Weather Service: TORNADO WARNING in this area until 2:30 PM CDT. Take shelter now in a basement or an interior room on the lowest floor of a sturdy building. If you are outdoors, in a mobile home, or in a vehicle, move to the closest substantial shelter and protect yourself from flying debris. Check media.

"Get the children to the cellar
Grab a bible if you can
Something wicked comes this way
To tear apart the land
Cut the horses from the stable
Put the fire out in the still
An evil wind is blowing through the hills"

"Blowing Through the Hills"
Recorded by Jason Boland

Writer: Jason Philip Boland

Day 15: Wednesday, August 11

Here is a trivia question for you…do you know the difference between a tornado warning and a tornado watch?

I learned the difference the summer of 1984 when I was at Purdue taking summer classes and living in the dorm. One of the girls I would see every morning in the cafeteria was a meteorology student. She was taking a summer class and part of what they did was "Storm Chasing". If you aren't from the Midwest, you may not understand that term…but just think of the movie "Twister". She was part of a team that would track weather patterns and wait for tornadoes to develop.

- Tornado Watch—means conditions are favorable.

- Tornado Warning—means one has been spotted either in person or on radar. That message usually looks like this:

⚠ EMERGENCY ALERTS

Emergency Alert
National Weather Service: TORNADO
WARNING in this area until 2:30 PM CDT.
Take shelter now in a basement or an
interior room on the lowest floor of a sturdy
building. If you are outdoors, in a mobile
home, or in a vehicle, move to the closest
substantial shelter and protect yourself
from flying debris. Check media.

When you see the line "take shelter", it isn't a good sign.

I was driving eighty in a group of five cars, you could tell we all got the message above at the same time as we all slowed down together. I looked around and saw the clouds doing some scary stuff. All five cars were thinking the same thing, should we pull over and look for cover… or make a run for it?

We all decided about the same time to make a run for it and luckily got out before any tornado was spotted. Though as far as adventures go that would have been a big one.

I left Wisconsin without any plan. I had an agenda to see some stuff in Minneapolis, but with all the weather and internet and computer problems I had been having I didn't have a chance to make any decisions.

I am feeling good though.

I think I will keep driving.

I haven't heard from Thumper all day. I am sure he is busy. Yet, I am still getting some weird vibes about the whole thing.

It is a beautiful day though, and I am only a few hours from knocking another state off my list of states I have visited.

Fargo North Dakota…here I come.

Chapter 21

North Dakota:

Fargo and Feeling Great

"But last I checked this heart inside my chest
Is still beating
Well I guess it's not too late
What if today's the only day I got?
I don't wanna waste it if it's my last shot
No regrets, in the end
I wanna know I got no what ifs
I'm running till the road runs out
I'm lighting it up right here right now
No regrets, in the end
I wanna know I got no what ifs"

"What If"
Recorded by Matthew West

Writers: Matthew West, Ran Jackson, AJ Pruis

Still Day 15: Wednesday, August 11

It's 9:28 pm and I just pulled into Fargo, North Dakota. My plan was to stop here for the night but I decided that I wanted to see the Corn Palace in South Dakota, thanks to Kim's suggestion. In order to do that and still get the other stops I want to make, I will have to drive a bit farther. It isn't a problem because I feel great. I mean really great. Better than I have in a long time. I can't believe that I have been driving for 12 hours. Even with stops to walk and stretch I never thought I would be able to do that again.

I have surprised myself by how long I am driving in the quiet. No music. None of the CDs I bought in Steubenville. None of the books on tape. Just me and my thoughts. Of course, I have a lot to think about.

I am still in shock over all that has happened but the strange feelings are getting stronger. I know that something isn't right and I am afraid that I have done something wrong. Pushed too hard. Wanted too much. Mile after mile I replay our text conversations in my mind. I am pretty sure it is over, and I am devastated, but I am also feeling a release. A freedom I haven't felt in a long time. So long in fact, that I didn't even recognize what it was. Each mile that passes I am more and more at peace. Stronger.

11:30 pm, I do finally hear from Thumper. Something was wrong, I felt it coming. I don't know what it is and there is nothing I can do. He says it isn't me, he says I can still text him but I think I need to just step back and give him some room. I want him to know how much these last few days have meant to me. I want him to know how our conversations have changed me. I want him to know that I would wait another thirty-seven years if I needed to and that I will always be here. Just like the letters I wrote him years ago the words just come out wrong. And now it is late. And I am tired. And it is pitch black. There are no other cars, no exits for a hotel or a bathroom or a break.

I am feeling very alone. And for the first time on this trip, I feel a twinge of panic. I can find no town or stop on my GPS. At all. Nowhere.

Facebook Post
Thursday, August 12, 12:27 AM

Not the best decision I ever made. The problem with driving until you get tired in South Dakota Is when you get tired there's no place to stop

I text a few people to see if they are awake and can get online and help me but the time difference does not work in my favor.

Finally, relief. Up ahead is Watertown, South Dakota. There are four hotels there.

I pull into the Hampton Inn parking lot and go inside. They are fully booked. AND have no idea if any of the other hotels have rooms.

I text a friend to let her know what is going on just in case I go missing in the middle of the night.

Text Message
12:50 AM

"Crap. Finally found a hotel and they are full. I might be sleeping in the parking lot."

I park my car next to a camper in the Walmart parking lot next door and start looking for the phone numbers for the other hotels…trying to come to terms with the fact that I may be sleeping in my car tonight.

Facebook Post
Thursday, August 12, 1:02 AM

Jean Tillery is at Country Inn & Suites by Radisson, Watertown, SD.

4th time's a charm. Good thing, I didn't want to sleep in the parking lot.

Next time I want to "drive farther" remind me to check how far I HAVE to go to get a room.

I got the very last room.

When Donna at the hotel said they had one room left I told her I would be there in three minutes and not to give it away. As I pulled into the parking lot, a truck was pulling in also. We both looked at each other and it was kind of a race to see who could get parked and to the hotel desk first.

As we all ran through the door at the same time, with the same panicked looks on our faces, she laughed and said "Don't worry guys, I have rooms for each of you". Seems we both called about the same time and luckily, we each got a room.

St. Michael was watching out for me once again. I made the decision that from now on I will just let God take over and will do nothing more than show up and be open to whatever He has got for me. No matter what happens going forward this trip has been worth it.

Chapter 22

South Dakota:
Sunflowers and Badlands

"Me I've been lookin' for you baby, I've been lookin' for you baby

I've been lookin' for you baby, I've been lookin' for you baby

All night long, all night long, all night long

I've been lookin' for you baby"

"El Cerrito Place"
Recorded by Charlie Robison

Writer: Keith Gattis

Day 16: Thursday, August 12

Sooooooo glad to wake up in a bed. Yesterday was crazy. I can't believe that I made it. I have been fighting my health for so long…even the smallest tasks were overwhelming and I never had the energy, I never had the stamina and I never would have been able to push myself like that…and recover.

There is a new excitement about this trip. I seem to have turned a corner. What that meant, I wasn't sure but I was ready to see how much I could challenge myself.

When I was bringing in my bags last night I found a penny on the floor, right next to the dresser. Now for most people that wouldn't mean much, but it has deep meaning for me.

When my kids were young, I taught them about Mary, the Mother of Jesus. I told them that as Jesus's Mother, Mary was also their "Mother" and when they found a penny on the ground that was a reminder that Mary was watching over them and bringing their prayers to Jesus. After my mother died it became my mom watching over them.

My kids grew up, but my belief that my mom would leave me coins to find so I knew she was watching me, and praying for me never stopped. I always find a penny when I need one…and if the need is exceptionally strong, I will find a dime or a quarter. Over and over again, in places you would not normally find money and in a time where there aren't many coins in use…they are there.

I picked the penny up and put it somewhere special, and thanked her for watching over me last night.

Downstairs at breakfast, I ran into the guys that made it to the hotel when I did last night. They were on their way to CA for work and with them was their dog. We ate together and shared pet stories and travel stories.

My great mood came to an abrupt halt. When I woke up that morning, I went to text my friend to let her know I did finally get a hotel room last night and that all was well and saw that it wasn't Terri that I texted, but Thumper. I saw that the text was read so I apologized.

Text Message

"Sorry, that was supposed to be sent to someone else. But since I am here...good morning! I hope you have a wonderful day, or at least you are able to find wonderful moments in it."

I soon had the proof that things had changed when that text didn't go through as an i-message but as a text message. (My youngest had to explain to me that that means I was blocked from his phone).

I was sad but not surprised. I felt it coming. I didn't have time to dwell on it at the moment, I had lots of ground to cover today and needed to get myself moving.

Facebook Post
Thursday, August 12, 11:06 AM

Epic Living with Jean is at Buffalo Ridge Country Store. Sioux Falls, SD

I can't NOT stop, right?

Buffalo jerky in the cooler.

#epicroadtrip

Just like my mom, I love a cool roadside stop, I needed a bathroom and this sign looked interesting…and it was. I had to get some buffalo jerky, the perfect road trip snack and I was enthralled by the eclectic merchandise in the store, but the true gem of this place was out back, and sadly it wasn't open that day…but I will be back someday to check it out.

What is so cool back behind a roadside jerky store that I would want to go back to the middle of South Dakota for? The Buffalo Ridge Ghost Town (1880 Cowboy Town). I was intrigued when I walked out back to take a look, but when I checked it out online it was even better.

The online article I found had this to say about it, "The town, despite its name, was built in the 1960s -- maybe -- by Dean Songstadt, his friend Bill Jorgenson, and two other guys whose names Dean either can't remember or just doesn't want to say. Dean and his son Brad run 1880 Cowboy Town (later renamed Buffalo Ridge Ghost Town). Dean is a cautious man, a little hard of hearing, and wary of people who ask too many questions.

There is no question, however, that he and his partners have built something really special: a totally automated Wild West town populated only by robots."

After reading about how cool it was, I was devastated that it wasn't open. (check out the online resource list for a link to the article)

A little farther down the road, I have to stop again, and luckily there is a rest stop when I need it. My dad used to tease me and say that by the time I died I would have stopped at every rest stop in the country. I can't help it. I travel with a cooler of my refillable water bottles. Hydration is important after all.

This particular rest area has a massive concrete tipi. There is a matching tipi at the rest stop on the other side of the interstate, and they are known as "Whitwan's Wigwams" named after the architect Ward Whitwam who designed them. They are landmarks in South Dakota and are on the National Register of Historic Places. Each one has 8 12x18 concrete lodge poles standing 56 feet high and weighing 6.5 tons. The base of the tipi is 35 feet in diameter. It is a sight to see, and worth the stop because you can't get a feel for the massive size unless you are close.

I ended up sitting there enjoying the sun, the beauty and the peace, and the openness for almost an hour. I am enjoying not having a schedule and being able to sit. It occurs to me that this trip was never meant to be about work, it was a chance for me to rediscover myself. To heal, and to dig through all the emotions that were bombarding me. I had spent so many years being everything to everyone that I had lost what it meant to be me. Now was the time to 'find' me, and I knew that this trip was going to be the first step in doing that.

Once again St. Michael knew I needed him and he reached out to me via a billboard sign advertising "The Fatima Family Shrine".

Who would imagine that in Alexandria, South Dakota, just off Interstate 90 and only fifteen minutes from my Corn Palace destination is a Marian shrine, located next to the Catholic parish of St. Mary of Mercy.

At the base of the Fatima Family Shrine are soil and rock from the exact place next to the oak tree where the Virgin Mary appeared to the three children in Portugal. The shrine features chapels made of South Dakota granite with Portuguese marble statues. One has the Holy Family, another one, Jesus, and one has the angel as he appeared to the children.

Off to the side of the shrine is a huge statue of St. Michael, his foot on the serpent and his spear up ready to slay the demon. It was as if he was saying, "Don't worry, I've got your back. God has sent me to watch over and protect you. You do what needs to be done"

I was only there a short time, but I left with the understanding that no matter what had happened up to now, this trip was about something bigger than I could imagine. I knew I needed to get out of the way and let it happen.

Still Day 16: Thursday, August 12

If this trip was a play, this would be the start of Act 2. Honestly, I didn't realize how much shifted until I came back and began to write the story.

I first noticed it when I got to the Corn Palace. Seriously. That is a place. Located in Mitchell, South Dakota, it is visited by 500,000 people each year. It is a venue for concerts, sporting events and community activities and it is made of corn. Well, more accurately, the entire building is decorated in corn. They use 12 different colors of corn grown locally and every ear is cut in half lengthwise and individually nailed to the wall to create a mural.

Each year the exterior murals are re-designed by local artists following a certain theme. The theme this year is "Stay Here, Play Here", but as my new friend, Bill, who was working the information desk told me, the corn murals are stripped by the end of August and the new ones are usually completed by the first of October.

Bill gave me the lowdown on the Corn Palace, and actually went and got me a chair so I could sit and chat with him. It was a slow day, he said. He also gave me a pile of maps and brochures and had many suggestions of what I needed to add to my trip. I think I could have done the entire #epicRoadtrip in South Dakota there was so much to see and do. Bill also had a suggestion for lunch… which was my next stop.

Facebook Post
Thursday, August 12, 1:14 PM

Epic Living with Jean is at The World's Only Corn Palace. Mitchell, SD

Again…I had to. This one is for you @kwepub

#prettycorny

#ichoseepic

#ichosetowander

#epicRoadtrip

#notgoingtostop

Facebook Post
Thursday, August 12, 1:26 PM

If it wasn't for the sucky winters, I could live in SD.

Trying to decide what's next.

Custer State Park?

Deadwood, SD

Badlands National Park?

Tell me what you think.

First thing I need to do is find a freaking hotel for tonight. 😫

#notdoingthatagain

#wontstop

I ran across the street to grab lunch, pour over my information and make some plans. The first of which was a hotel. I was NOT going through what I did last night. I asked 1000 questions of the waitress and got the attention of the man at the table next to me. He had some great stories and asked me a lot of questions about my trip. By the time lunch was over I had a lot of great ideas, but made the decision that I was heading to Badlands National Park. AND I also had a free lunch. Turns out the guy I was talking to bought my lunch. Now that was cool. I didn't get his name or I would give him a proper thank you. It's 2:30 pm but I am not stopping yet.

Still Day 16: Thursday, August 12

Heading West. Interstate 90 shows me 2 of my favorite things. Wind turbines (we have already had THAT conversation) and sunflowers! Miles and miles of sunflowers on both sides of the highway.

Sunflowers are a significant contributor to the state's economy. The crop is used mostly for its oil and its seed products. They aren't a big provider of cut flowers, but I do wish I had time to stop and find a place to buy some.

It is 3 hours between the Corn Palace and Badlands National Park…and I am still handling it like a pro. I am feeling amazing and fueled by the excitement and energy of the road. You can catch a glimpse of the Badlands' geographic formations from miles away. Over the years I have had a chance to visit many National Parks but this is my first time at the Badlands. I wasn't very familiar with the park, but I had heard the term "badlands" before but wasn't sure where or when.

Turns out, the word can mean 2 different things. Badlands with a capital "B" means the park, badlands with a lowercase 'b' is a geological term that describes the terrain that looks like what you see at the park, typically soft sedimentary rocks that erode easily. There are badland formations all over the country in places like Wyoming, Utah, North Dakota, Colorado, and Nebraska.

The Badlands have a number of different rock types dating back as far as 75 million years: sandstone, siltstones, mudstones, claystones, limestones, volcanic ash and shale, each coming from different sources and giving the unique layered look of the park. The park is 244,000 acres and contains one of the world's richest fossil beds. I entered the Northeast Entrance and drove the Badlands Loop Road (Hwy 240) through the park. It was thirty-nine miles of two-lane paved road that takes you through some of the most scenic areas of the park.   There were many places to park and get out and several trails that were accessible. My first stop was right outside the park to get a photo of the park entrance sign. There was a group of bikers that had pulled up at the same time and asked me to take a picture for them. Since the Motorcycle Rally in Sturgis was going on there were a lot of bikers…that made it tougher to find hotel rooms which I will learn quickly…but how cool it must be to see that view from a bike. I only stopped a few times, it had been a long day, but the loop drive really gave me a feel for the different types of formations and grassland of the park. I promised myself I would be back someday when I got healthy and could hike some of the trails. I would also love to do some of the astronomy programs. I can imagine how huge the sky must look from there at night.

Still Day 16: Thursday, August 12

One more stop and I am getting there right on time. In the summer of 2002, Dan and I did the cattle drive for the third time. We drove in from Chicago where we had buried my mother. Dan drove with me and the kids, but after the cattle drive, he flew back home to work and I drove home with the kids…stopping as many places as I could with a 2-year-old, a 6-year-old, and a 9-year-old. Mt. Rushmore was one of the places and it has been on my dream list to go back and that is exactly where I was headed.

Mt. Rushmore National Monument is a colossal sculpture carved into the granite face of the mountain in the Black Hills near Keystone, South Dakota. Sculptor Gutzon Borglum designed and oversaw the project from 1927 to 1941 with his son Lincoln. The sculpture features sixty-foot-tall heads of four American Presidents, George Washington, Thomas Jefferson, Theodore Roosevelt and Abraham Lincoln. They were chosen to represent the nation's birth, growth, development and preservation and it attracts more than 2,000,000 people annually.

My goal was to get there in time to get settled before dark because I wanted to see the monument lit up. It is a powerful image during the day, but it is magical at night. After parking, it was a bit of a hike to get to the viewing area. It had been a long day and it was after 8:00 pm. There was a good crowd but still able to space out away from each other. I was surprised at the number of foreigners there, and I lost count of the number of languages I heard.

At the base of the monument is the Avenue of Flags, a feature that displays the flags of all fifty states, one district, three territories and two commonwealths of the US. The avenue of flags leads up to an outdoor open amphitheater, with a lot of stairs going down so beware. I took it slow, but found an open area not too far down and settled in to look for a hotel while it got dark.

Funny story…I was having problems finding a hotel (big surprise huh?). I was already tired and wasn't sure how long I would be able to drive after I left Mt. Rushmore. I was getting a bit…testy. They made an announcement that the "Lighting Ceremony" would begin at 9:00, starting with a Ranger talk. My first thought was…just light the stupid thing. I am hungry and tired and grumpy and don't need to hear a Ranger talk.

I then reminded myself that I was supposed to be "open to the experience" so I relaxed and said "Give me whatever You got God" and He gave me His best.

The Ranger (a woman) gave the most amazing talk. She started out "When you think of America, what are some words that come to mind? The words freedom, democracy and sacrifice are a few, but what about the word experiment? America's beginnings have often been referred to as the great experiment but we don't always think in those terms. Yet before our country's constitution was written, no system of government in the world existed quite like this one. America, in its essence, began as an experiment and is an experiment that is still ongoing to this day". I was hooked. Her talk was only about 8 minutes long but it was powerful (I posted a link to a video and the transcript of it in the resource area on my website). We sang the National Anthem and said the Pledge of Allegiance (I am a sucker for both), but my favorite part was that they invited any active or retired military to the stage. There were a lot of Sturgis bikers in the crowd and many of them were servicemen and women so about 25 people headed to the stage to a standing ovation and loud applause. Together they lowered the flag. There was a short video about each of the four Presidents and as the video finishes, the lights slowly come up on the monument. It was a moving ceremony and worth the thirty minutes it took. I left a little teary and thankful that I let go of the frustration and enjoyed the evening. AND I did find a hotel, only one and a half hours away.

Chapter 23

Wyoming:
My Spirit Place

"I knew in my limb, when I was a kid
It'd be hard to ever be still.
'Cause there's so much to see
And It all calls to me.
I don't believe
I ever will stop this
Wandering, wandering, wandering round"

"Wandering"
Recorded by Walt Wilkins

Writers: Walt Wilkins and Drew Kennedy

Day 17: Friday, August 13

I woke up in Sundance, WY this morning. This hotel was the perfect example of just how different things out west are. I made the reservation while at Mt. Rushmore last night. By the time I got to the Deer Lodge Motel, it was after midnight. I was surprised when I saw that the office was closed.

As I pulled up, I began to worry I would REALLY have to sleep in my car this time. It was all good though. There was a note on the door of the office with my name on it. It said, "Thank you for choosing the Bear Lodge and Deer Lodge for your lodging accommodations, Jean Tillery. Your key is in the black drop box next to the office door located in the courtyard here at the Bear Lodge Motel. Please fill out the form included with your key and finish checking in in the morning. Thank you, Management."

Seriously? Who does this? I have stayed in a lot of hotels/motels/Inns in my life and I have never seen this. It made me happy, not just because I had a bed to sleep in, but the trust and generosity was a huge change from what I saw back home.

Needless to say, I slept REALLY well last night.

Facebook Post
Thursday, August 12, 11:06 AM

56 years ago I was born in Houston Texas.

That day, my parents got a call from Catholic Charities of Galveston Diocese saying that their daughter was here.

I used to love to hear Al Hardey tell me the story of

how he went with my parents to pick me up. How they were scared to get too invested and they hadn't bought anything for me so they had to stop at the store on the way. How my dad drove the whole way to the hospital with the windshield wipers on even though it hadn't rained in weeks.

This day, I have so many people to thank...my birth mother who so selflessly placed me for adoption so that I could have a chance for a better life.

To my family and friends who have been with me and supported me, laughed and cried with me.

To my customers and clients and business partners who have helped me to build a business that I love and gives me the opportunity to change the world.

To my husband who doesn't bat an eye when I tell him that I'm going takeoff for 5 1/2 weeks and drive across the country.

I love you all, and for my birthday this year, I'm asking you for something really special. There is nothing that I need but I ask for this...

Take a moment today to say a prayer, in whatever matter or means that you do. Whether it's a daily rosary, a Mass, quiet prayer, song, meditation or just sending good thoughts.

Right now, I have a long list of prayer intentions that I keep on my phone and I ask you to say a prayer for me, and for all those on my list who need it. Health issues, family issues, relationship issues, addiction issues, painful lives, and broken spirits...there is some of everything on that list. AND if you are having difficulties and NEED a prayer, please add it to the cloud of offering. (And feel free to reach out to me to be added to my personal list)

I have seen the power of prayer and I know we can do some amazing things when we link together.

This is one of my favorite prayers...I believe everyone has a guardian angel, but I have always had a personal attachment to Saint Michael.

St Michael the Archangel is referenced in the Old Testament and has been part of Christian teachings since the earliest times. He acts as the defender of the Church and chief opponent of Satan and is the intercessor between God and His people.

He had been a constant companion on this trip as almost every day I have been gone he shows himself to me.

Thank you for having patience with all my long tough posts lately. Hours in a car by yourself leads to some pretty heavy meditation.

I love you all.

———————————-

PRAYER TO SAINT MICHAEL THE ARCHANGEL

Saint Michael the Archangel,

defend us in battle.

Be our defense against the wickedness and snares of the Devil.

May God rebuke him, we humbly pray,

and do thou,

O Prince of the heavenly hosts,

by the power of God,

Cast into hell Satan,

and all the evil spirits,

who prowl about the world

seeking the ruin of souls.

Amen.

#epicFaith

#epicRoadtrip

#thepowerofprayer

#wontstop

It's my birthday. My first thought is maybe, just maybe, Thumper will reach back out to me. Not that he knows it's my birthday, we hadn't talked about it.

He did tell me that I could still text him, so yesterday, I did. I sent him a picture from Badlands and one from Mt. Rushmore. Neither of them went through. Nevertheless…I won't stop. Stop trying or stop hoping.

Text Message

"Happy Birthday to me. This is the second time you have been the best present that I ever could have gotten.

I have really enjoyed all the conversations that we had. You are smart, funny and caring. I know you need time and space but I will continue reading and re-reading them. You need to know that I'm not going away. I don't want anything. I am not asking

for anything but I won't stop loving you. I won't stop waiting for you. Even if I have to wait 37 more years."

Again, the text doesn't go through, but I can't think about that now…today is a BIG day. I am up early and moving quickly. I need to get to Yellowstone by tonight but today is only about one thing. Devils Tower.

This will be the third time I have visited. The first was when I was young. 1972 I believe. There is a picture of me there with my parents in a box somewhere. The second time was when my kids and I were driving home from Montana in 2002. I had my youngest in a backpack while we hiked around and climbed over the rocks at the base of the tower. I have no pictures from that day because 8 rolls of film from that trip got destroyed while being processed. When that happened, I said I would be back and now, nineteen years later, I am just thirty minutes away.

There has always been something about this monument that calls to me. Just like Roy Neary, the character that Richard Dreyfuss plays in the 1977 movie "Close Encounters of the Third Kind" there has been a pull to come back and as I was planning this trip I was determined to be here on my birthday and hike the entire base of the monument. And now I am heading there. I am not sure how long it will take me to hike. I am feeling better, feeling amazing actually, but I haven't done a lot of walking yet and I have no idea if I will be able to make it work.

Devil's Tower is a laccolithic butte composed of igneous rock. It was formed underground from molten rock that intruded into the existing sedimentary rock layers around 30 million years ago. Over the (millions) of years, ancient rivers washed away the softer sedimentary rocks leaving behind the harder igneous rock. The tower is still emerging as the Belle Fourche River continues to wash away the softer rock.

It became the first National Monument, proclaimed on September 24, 1906 by President Roosevelt by authority of the newly created Antiquities Act.

The tower rises 1,267 feet above the Belle Fourche River. It is 867 feet from the base to the summit which is why it attracts rock climbers from all over the world. It is the world's largest example of columnar jointing (which you can see clearly in the photos, check them out in the Resources section of my website). It is also a sacred place to over twenty Native American tribes, who know it as "Bear Lodge or Bear Tipi". (The name Devil's Tower is said to come from a mistranslation of the Native American name).

Parking is extremely limited and was interesting with all the tourists in big motorhomes. Just like Badlands NP, there were a lot of motorcycles here as they were sightseeing before/after their trip to Sturgis. I spent a few minutes resting at the visitor's center where I talked to 2 women who were finishing their picnic lunch at the pavilion and asked me to take their picture. They were traveling from Sturgis on bikes and as we chatted, they told me that they started coming to Sturgis over 20 years ago. Their husbands had grown up together and served in the military together and the four of them would meet up in Sturgis every year. Both of the women had lost their husbands, but they continued to meet up for a few days every year to continue the tradition. They wished me Happy Birthday, and even gave me a cupcake then sent me off on my Birthday hike.

The "Tower Trail" is a paved trail that begins at the parking lot at the Visitors Center. Starting at the parking lot the hike is 1.8 miles with the loop around the tower itself 1.3 miles. There are stretches that have some mild to moderate elevation changes so in my condition it was challenging. I passed a family of seven that were taking the trail with their grandfather. When I stopped at one of the many benches along the trail to rest and take pictures, the group passed me. A little while later I passed them while they rested. It was back and forth the entire hike. That was good for me because it gave me some motivation as well as a way to pace myself. I wanted to get a photo with them at the end, but I stopped to talk to some climbers and they were gone by the time I was done.

Climbers? Yes. I got to meet a group that was just getting ready to go up, as well as a group that had just finished. They told me that the climb is difficult but can be done by a beginner who has some experience as long as they are with a certified rock guide who knows the tower. I can honestly say that is one thing NOT on my Dream List!

The ascent normally takes four to six hours, but during busy seasons it can take longer because of the 'lines' of people on the climb. The group pointed out a friend who was up on the wall as we talked. They also told me you can climb up and camp on the top if you are able to snag one of the few campsites there.

There are two times of the year when the tower is not open to climb. In April certain routes are closed to protect the nesting sites of falcons.

There is also a voluntary ban during the month of

June to allow for the spiritual ceremonies of the Native Americans. Along the trail you see bundles of colorful "prayer cloths" that are tied on branches of the trees. They may represent a person making an offering, a request, or simply in remembrance of a person or place.

I read this in the park brochure: "It is important to note a key difference between American Indian religions and many other contemporary religions (referred to as "western" or "near eastern" religions): a sense of place dominates the religion of American Indians, as opposed to the sense of time that dominates many western religions. Instead of a focus of chronological events and the order in which they are presented,

American Indian religion focuses on a place and the significant events that are connected with that location. Although Western religions have their important places, they do not hold the level of sacredness associated with the important places of American Indian religions."

Different tribes have different stories of how the Tower came to be. My favorite version, and the one I remember from my very first visit is from the Kiowa and Lakota. A group of girls went out to play and were spotted by several giant bears, who began to chase them. In an effort to escape the bears, the girls climbed atop a rock, fell to their knees, and prayed to the Great Spirit to save them. Hearing their prayer, the Great Spirit made the rock rise from the ground towards the heavens so that the bears could not reach the girls.

The bears, in an effort to climb the rock, left deep claw marks in the sides, which had become too steep to climb. Those are the marks which appear today on the sides of

Devil's Tower. When the girls reached the sky, they were turned into the stars of the Pleiades. I have loved Native American history and culture since I was young, maybe that is part of my draw to Devil's Tower.

The hike took me about two hours and was amazing, exhausting, invigorating, and physically demanding, but the reward of finishing the challenge I had set was just what I needed. The spectacular views along the way added the perfect touch and made this the best birthday present I could have given myself.

By the time I got back to my car, there were people directing traffic in the parking lot. The crowds had grown and the number of large campers made it a logistical nightmare.

One of the ladies helping to direct the traffic came over to check and make sure I was okay. I had been sitting in my car catching my breath and changing out of my hiking shoes. She introduced herself and explained that she was a member of a local motorcycle group and each year they volunteered at the monument during the ten days of Sturgis to help direct all the extra traffic and help in getting people parked. She asked about me and I explained my road trip and how I was on a mission to spread the message of "Dreaming" but that my trip had gone sideways with all the emotional stuff that happened. She asked me if she could pray with me, and right there, in the middle of the parking lot, she brought me to tears with her general concern and love for me…a total stranger. She asked me if there was any intention that I had that she could continue to pray for, and I asked her to pray for my newly found son. Pray that he is safe and happy and that somehow, we can build some kind of connection between us. Even if it is a tiny one. She left me with a huge hug and 2 small handmade gifts. What a way to spend a birthday.

It's a 7-hour drive to Yellowstone and I need to be there tonight.

Facebook Post
Friday, August 13

Thank you Devil's Tower National Monument

You were everything I hoped and more.

I will be back soon!!!!

When my husband and I drove to Montana in 2002 I was enthralled by the changing landscape. From fields to plains to mountains. I was getting that feeling today. There is something magical about looking out in the distance and seeing the mountains appear...even when you are far away.

Facebook Post
Friday, August 13

Getting some miles in today. I love the way the landscape is changing as we go through Wyoming; we're starting to see mountains off in the distance will be in Yellowstone tonight.

I am still traveling in silence. For someone who loves music like I do that is surprising to me. Yet my thoughts are keeping me company and with each mile, I am feeling more grounded and stronger. I am reconnecting with parts of me I haven't seen in a while. I have shed tears. A lot of tears. That's ok. Tearing down the walls that I have built is a slow painful process but the perfect thing to be doing while covering all these miles.

Facebook Post
Friday, August 13

Today was a BIG drive day. I had a wonderful morning at Devils Tower, Wyoming, and made the trek to Yellowstone National Park.

The drive was long... but amazingly beautiful.

Pictures coming soon!

Checked in to my favorite Three Bears Lodge I am extremely lucky to be spending my 2nd year in a row here.

Chapter 24

Montana:
I Should've Been A Cowboy

"I should've been a cowboy
I should've learned to rope and ride
Wearing' my six-shooter, ridin' my pony on a cattle drive"

"Should've Been A Cowboy"
Recorded by Toby Keith

Written by Toby Keith

Still Day 17: Friday, August 13

Facebook Post

Jean Tillery is at Three Bear Lodge and Restaurant

West Yellowstone, MT

I am totally overwhelmed with all my birthday wishes AND prayer requests as well as prayer commitments.

It was weird to spend most of the day alone driving which was one of many reasons I needed all that love and as usual my tribe comes through for me. Each one of you is something special to me.

Now off to bed. I have an early date with a herd of bison...

#WontStop

My schedule for this trip is pretty loose. Actually, there are only three things that I HAVE to make sure I make happen. The first was the conference in Ohio. The second is to be at the airport in Bozeman Montana to pick up my husband when he flies in tomorrow.

For now, I have some time to play in Yellowstone. I got to the hotel late last night but still, I am up early and ready to head to the park. Another thing that has been a big surprise this trip? The number of sunrises I have seen. It is incredible. Especially since a mere six months ago, I was sleeping twenty+ hours a day. I have been up late driving, up late reading or writing and still manage to get up early. There is something to be said for handing your life over to God and letting him make the decisions.

This is my third trip to Yellowstone and my first trip alone. I am excited about having no agenda, no schedule. I plan on making the most of my very short time here.

Yellowstone is our country's first National Park. It is 2.2 million acres which makes it bigger than Rhode Island and Delaware combined. There are more than 10,000 hydrothermal features in Yellowstone, the four types of thermals are geysers, hot springs, mud pots and fumaroles. It is home to more than 500 active geysers, more than half the world's geyser count.

It is also home to the largest concentration of mammals in the lower forty-eight states with over sixty-five species. You can observe wildlife up close, sometimes VERY up-close.

There are also 290 waterfalls and 1000 miles of hiking trails with over 1800 known archaeological sites within the park.

There are also five park entrances with over 450 miles of road. I have never spent more than a few days here, and I have always stayed outside of the park in West Yellowstone since that is the easiest coming from Bozeman Montana. There are nine hotels in the park though, as well as twelve campgrounds, so my next trip will be longer and I will be staying inside the park.

There are many amazing things in Yellowstone, but two of the most popular are the wildlife and Old Faithful. If you don't have the option of seeing Old Faithful in person, then check out Yellowstone's live feed. They have 9 cameras around the park.

The thing that is great about the wildlife is that they are out and walking around the park. You can check with any of the Ranges to see in what area of the park the wildlife is being seen. In 2020, when we were at Yellowstone and I was very sick, it was nice to be able to see the wildlife from the car, sometimes they will come right up to you.

In 1998, during our first trip to Yellowstone, Dan and I were hiking to a river for him to flyfish and there were bison just hanging out, right in the middle of the trail. Needless to say, we went OFF the trail and circled WAY around them.

Saturday morning, I got in the park a little after 6:00 AM. I found a place to park and just watched the sun come up over the mountains. The mist was rising from the water as the air was warming. I, of course, wanted to get closer to get a better photo of the water so I did something I haven't done in a long time. I climbed out to the bed of the river, scrambling over rocks to get there. I can't remember how long it has been since I could trust my body to be able to do things like that. It was a huge win for me. I spent the next few hours driving and stopping. Walking and resting. I put away my phone and just experienced the park and everything that nature was telling me. For someone who is very tied to communication that was new for me.

Facebook Post

Spent over 3 hours in the park this morning. Today is all about downloading and editing pictures, and doing a lot of writing and posting. Oh, and laundry. Hoping that I can accomplish that all while poolside.

Get ready to be bombarded, but in the meantime here's something special for you.

#epicSunrise

#yellowstonenationalpark

#epiclivingwithjean

#epicroadtrip

#WontStop

Still Day 17: Friday, August 13

I started the day with a sunrise drive into the park.

Facebook Post
Sunday, August 15

My last day in Yellowstone.

I went into the park to watch the sunrise. I left my phone and my camera and everything in the hotel because I just wanted to spend a moment enjoying it all to myself.

I love the symbolism of the sunrise and the new day. It's a new day to work on becoming the best version of ourself. It's a new day to enjoy the people in the things around us. It's a new day of endless possibilities.

There are times when it is hard to remember that we have endless opportunities to make that day #epic, but somehow, in the huge magnitude if the mountains I feel like I can do anything.

#epiceveryday

#epiclivingwithjean

#yellowstonenationalpark

#yellowstonenationalpark

Sunday means Mass and there is a great church in West Yellowstone, Our Lady of the Pines. It is exactly what you would think a church there would look like. An "A" frame building, lots of wood, open ceiling, and rustic beauty.

It is almost inconceivable that last Sunday I was attending Mass in Chicago. A lot has happened since then. I have traveled a lot of miles since then.

After Mass, it is back to the hotel to organize and reload the car then a quick trip to Bozeman to pick up my husband. As I waited in the terminal for him, I thought about how far I had come since the start of the trip. Not only physically better but mentally. I was really thinking that he would come off the plane and take one look and notice a change in me. I was sure that I looked as different as I felt.

When he landed the only thing on his mind was getting the vacation started. First thing on the agenda was lunch.

Bozeman is a growing town that blends outdoor adventure with a lively cultural scene. Surrounded by the Gallatin and Bridger Mountain Ranges, it is a haven for outdoor enthusiasts, offering world-class hiking, skiing, hunting and fly-fishing opportunities. It has a charming downtown area with shops, art galleries and a thriving music scene. It also has lots of eating choices, from fun, funky local eateries, to upscale restaurants. Today's lunch was provided by Copper Whiskey Bar and Grill. Their slogan is "come for the food and stay for the whiskey". The food was amazing and the bartender was great. We sat and talked to the couple next to us until we were almost late for stop number two. We were off to Wild Joe's Coffee Spot to meet Tessy Lou Williams.

Tessy Lou is a singer/songwriter who splits her time between Montana and Texas. She is the daughter of musicians and after overcoming her stage fright she began performing at the historic Pony Bar in Pony, Montana. I met her in Texas a few years before and was excited that we were both in Bozeman at the same time and she was able to meet up with me. My #epicStories podcasts are short and light so we were done quickly and back on the road for a short drive to Ennis Montana.

We were heading there so my husband could do some fly fishing before the cattle drive. Ennis is a small town, population 917, and the locals refer to it as a "small drinking town with a fishing problem". As a resort community, the town attracts an influx of seasonal tourists because of its location in the heart of prime fishing and hunting areas. The Madison River, which skirts the east side of Ennis, is a blue-ribbon trout stream, and the surrounding mountains provide excellent hunting for a variety of big game animals. We are spending the night at the Rainbow Valley Lodge which is cool enough that I wish we could stay longer. The owners, Ed and Jeanne Williams have a well-maintained, beautiful place that feels like home.

Day 20: Monday, August 16

Facebook Post
Monday, August 16, 2021

The Madison River where Dan is fly fishing today. They hit the water early because fishing stops at 2:00 because of the Red Owl Law.

— in Ennis, MT.

Now, to be clear, I thought it was a "Red Owl Law" and something to do with endangering Owls. BUT after I asked around about it, it turns out that it is known as the "Hoot Owl". What that means, is that there are restrictions to fishing between the hours of 2:00 PM and 12:00 AM because of drought conditions.

Why is it called Hoot Owl you ask? I did. It is because fishing is only allowed during the cooler hours of the day from Midnight to 2:00 PM which are the hours when the hoot owls are typically active. Makes perfect sense.

I dropped my husband off with the fishing guide and then headed back to the hotel for a leisurely breakfast and then loaded up the car. I had a meeting scheduled that I couldn't miss, so I headed to the public library where Dan will meet me when he is done. I love libraries. Is it weird that when I travel I often check out the local library? It is a great place to work, has free WIFI and it's quiet. The fact that I am not distracted by a bed like I would be in my hotel room is a plus. And there are lots of books.

Facebook Post
Monday, August 16, 2021

Jean Tillery is at Madison Valley Public Library

Ennis, MT

Meeting on the road.

Sandra Yancey's Sip, Tip and Talk.

Learning from the best.

"Building a business is hard....

Being broke is harder."

#choseepic

#liftasyouclimb

#epiclivingwithjean
#wontstop

I love that I have the ability to work anywhere. At least, anywhere with an internet connection. In between my meetings and client calls I back up more photos but then can't help but poke around in the books and see what is new and popular to read in Montana.

Still Day 20: Monday, August 16

From Ennis we head to Townsend Montana to meet up with the rest of the cattle drive guests. It is a short drive, just a little over an hour, but it seems like it is a world away.

This is our sixth cattle drive. In 1998, my husband and I had made summer plans with my parents, both my brothers and their wives to do an Alaskan cruise. My father developed some health issues that we couldn't find answers to and so that trip got canceled. Since we had saved up money for the trip, and never had a honeymoon, Dan and I decided to find an adventure of our own. It was going to be our ten-year anniversary, so we wanted something totally different.

There was no Google back then, but I did get online and found what sounded like the perfect vacation…Montana High Country Cattle Drive. The pictures showed a scene that looked like it was right out of a Larry McMurtry book. People on horseback pushing cattle through fields and mountain passes. They promised it was NOT a dude ranch experience. And I immediately signed us up.

When we landed in Bozeman that first trip, we ran into two other couples who were on the cattle drive with us. As we all stood in the baggage claim area, we couldn't help but notice a group of handsome men, all in matching pearl snap shirts and pressed jeans, with black cowboy hats and red bandanas grabbing luggage off the turnstile for people.

They were obviously part of some 'outfit', here to pick up their guests. As the 6 of us looked at each other we all thought the same thing…I hope those guys aren't from our trip. Just about that time, in walks an old cowboy wearing faded jeans and worn-out boots. He has a straw hat, a huge smile, and a piece of cardboard with the words "Cattle Drive" written in marker. He had a bit of a limp and when he came up to us, he said "Hi, my name is Hank, are you here for the cattle drive?" I couldn't help but smile back. I knew right then that this was going to be the trip of a lifetime.

And it was. So much so, that we signed up to come back the next summer even before we left Montana. Sadly, my father passed away the week of the trip that next summer so we couldn't go. I swore nothing was going to stop me from being there in 2000. Even after I found out I was pregnant with my third child. That summer I was there, 6 weeks before I was due. I didn't ride, obviously, but it was still the greatest vacation ever. We were back two years later, in 2002. That was after we buried my mother and drove from Chicago with the kids. In 2004 we were back once again, this time bringing some friends.

After that, life took over. Kids' sports and work kept us away, yet we stayed friends with the families that were involved in putting it on. The old guy Hank that picked us up that first day? He ended up moving to South Carolina and we became even closer, visiting each other often over the years.

In 2020, with the effects of COVID still interfering,

most of the cattle drive guests had to cancel and Hank called us up. He told us that there was plenty of space and that we should come back that summer.

He had continued to work with the outfitters helping with the drives every summer but he was getting older and his doctor told him it was time he stayed home. If this was going to be his last cattle drive, he wanted us to be there, and of course, if we had to social distance, Montana would be the best place to do that. I was too sick to ride, most days I would get up and watch everyone mount up and ride off and then I would go back to sleep.

This trip I was determined for more. Riding was still not an option but I will be moving, I will be more engaged, I will be a part of it all. Since I accomplished my challenge to myself to hike around Devil's Tower, this part of the trip I came up with a new challenge. The entrance to Battle Creek Ranch is at the top of a hill. When you pass through the gates, and over the cattle guard, it is a straight shot downhill to the Ranch House and our cabin. I told myself that I would hike up that hill at least 3 times while I was there. I am not sure exactly how far it was but it was a big challenge. One that I completed. AND I felt great about it.

Text Message
Tuesday, August 17

"I am not sure if you see or read these...I will be offline for a few days. I wish you could see this place. The beauty here at the ranch is stark. They are battling fires, drought and wind, but the people here are determined, and they are fighters. They are ranchers and farmers that have been on this land for hundreds

of years. They are really good people to be around right now."

The cattle drive has changed from when we used to come here. You are still doing real work; this is not a re-enactment for entertainment. It is a job that the ranch could do themselves in a day or two, but they got smart and started having guests PAY them to do the work.

Back then there were three drives. The first drive you are moving the cows and their calves from the ranch to the pasture up the mountain. The middle drive you move them up higher to fresh grass. The final drive you bring them back to the ranch.

During the early years, the drives were put on by a group of families all working together. There would be twenty or more guests. We would actually be gathering the cows and moving them quite a distance, staying on the trail each night. There would be large tents set up at each stop that would stay up all summer for the single people. Then small two-man tents would be set up and taken down at each stop for the couples. We would move the cows from one camp to the next and after we left, they would break down the camp, load up the cook trailer and supplies and set off to the next camp. It was quite an operation and took a lot of manpower, a lot of wranglers, and a lot of coordinating to pull it off.

Over the years things have changed, and the drive we did in 2020 and this year was completely at Battle Creek Ranch.

Each morning the team would mount up and gather the Battle Creek cattle and bring them back to the ranch. There is a lot about the old days I miss, but I have to say staying in a cabin with a bed, shower and toilet is really nice.

There may be fewer guests and a lot less cattle to move, but we are still doing the work that needs to be done. And Lary and Shelly Richtmyer, the ranch owners, are still treating us like kings.

I went to run errands with Shelly one day. One of our stops was a local Hutterite community to pick up meat and vegetables.

The Hutterites are a communal Anabaptist religious group, part of the larger Christian Radical Reformation movement that emerged in the 16th century. They are named after Jakob Hutter, a leader of the early movement.

Hutterite communities are known for their communal living arrangements, where members live and work together on collective farms. They share resources and live a simple lifestyle, emphasizing community over individual ownership. Hutterite colonies often include communal dining halls, schools, and workshops and they embrace certain modern technologies, such as tractors and electricity, as they believe in using tools that contribute to communal living and sustainability.

Shelly and I were able to go into a workshop where there was a large group of women of all ages sitting in a circle prepping vegetables. Shelly is here often and knows several of the women and I watch as they talk quietly catching up. I notice a quiet simplicity with the women there, but there are a lot of smiles and laughter.

Members typically wear traditional clothing, and the community follows a set of rules and guidelines outlined in their religious beliefs. They are a very private group but before we left the women all joined together to sing a song for us. Something they would often do while working. It was a special thing to witness and I felt honored that they would do that for us.

Day 22: Wednesday, August 18

Facebook Post

I have only a few minutes of internet. I left Battle Creek Ranch to come to Townsend, Montana to see if I could track down Gayle.

It is rainy and about 42 right now. But the good thing is hopefully this will put an end to the worst of the local fires and when this all passes, we should have a beautiful view of the mountains.

Battle Creek Ranch, where we're staying, is at an elevation of about 7000 feet. There's no cell service at the ranch, but if you're lucky you may be able to go up the hill to the front gate and catch a weak signal. So we're reachable if there's an emergency. ☺

Yesterday the team brought the first round of cattle into the ranch. And I've got some great videos but for now, I will leave you with these photos and I can't wait to fill you in on all the details.

Over the years I have learned a lot about ranching. This is hard work, and for the most part, they are doing it the same way they did it hundreds of years ago. Land management, extreme and unpredictable weather, water and lack of, livestock breeding techniques, nutrition and veterinary care, and just the cost of doing business means they need to be knowledgeable about a lot of different things.

Day 23: Thursday, August 19

The cattle "pairs" (a momma and her calf) have all been collected and brought to the ranch. Now comes my favorite part.

The cows are collected into a corral and all the calves are separated. A rider will go into the group of calves and rope a single one and bring him into a work area where there are teams of people set up in stations to brand them, ear tag them, give them their shots and if they are a male calf, castrate them. This procedure seems violent and cruel but in actuality, it benefits the animals as much as the ranchers. The teams work like a race car pit crew with each person having a job and the whole process takes less than two minutes.

Afterward, the calf bounces up and goes looking for his mother. There is skill involved in handling these calves without hurting them. AND without them hurting you.

Still Day 23: Thursday, August 19

I got a message today about a friend's son. I don't know the details, but the son is in the hospital after being shot 3 times. This was a dear friend I have known for years. Our kids grew up together and I love this boy like my own. As a parent, I am heartbroken and afraid.

I also come to a hard realization. Since there has been no more communication with Thumper, I would never know if something happened to him. It is one thing to step back and give him time and space…it is another to have to go back to wondering where he is and if something happened to him. I wonder if he would care if something happened to me?

Day 24: Friday, August 20

Today is my thirty-third wedding anniversary. That seems like such a huge number. It doesn't seem that long. When I sit back and think of all the stories we have, I realize how much we have crammed into our time together. I am lucky that he puts up with me and all my wild plans and adventures. The other notable thing about tonight is the huge full moon overhead. Montana's sky is a stargazing bonanza. At this altitude and with no other light interference there are millions of stars. Tonight is cloudy but the moon peeks through for a short time and it puts on a glorious show.

Still Day 24: Friday, August 20

Lazy day today. I get the car cleaned out and packed back up. Dan needs to get his boarding pass for his flight tomorrow, so we drive up the hill hoping to find some cell service. After a few days here with no internet, you realize how attached to technology we have become. I have had the chance to edit pictures and write a lot. I put the finishing touches on my first book, #epicMessages and it will be ready to turn over to my publisher when I get home. I take one last hike and manage to walk quite a bit down the road. I will miss this place. It has always been a special place for me. The people, the beauty, the memories.

During the old drives, Saturday night meant a barn dance, but with this small group, we are relaxing around the ranch house and listening to Hank sing and tell stories.

He gives us a special treat when he recites a few of his Cowboy poems.

Hank has been a part of these cattle drives since the beginning. He was the camp manager and chief entertainer. Almost every night was spent around the campfire while Hank played guitar. He is the consummate entertainer, and the true example of a renaissance man if there ever was one. His life and his stories could fill its own book, in fact, he is writing that story now. At ninety he has slowed down, but he is as sharp as ever. He no longer rides horses, but he is still helping out. He plays banjo now instead of guitar because of the arthritis in his hands. He can still quote his poems from memory and he still flirts with all the girls.

Like all the drives in the past, there is a very eclectic group of guests. Different ages, backgrounds and reasons to be here. We are not the only returning guests this trip. I love how we all come together as strangers and leave as friends. Working together tends to create a bond, and there are several people that we met on the cattle drives in the past that we are still connected to.

Text Message

It's my last day at Battle Creek Ranch. I'll be leaving tomorrow morning and heading back on the road. This has been such a great break.

There are some amazing guests on the drive. One mother and son in particular. His name is Daniel and his mother is battling some medical issues and wasn't able to ride, but she also had just a difficult time getting around in general. He took such wonderful care of her it was beautiful to watch. He would get

her a plate of food at each meal, would help her get around, and was just very attentive to her.

It blew me away on Tuesday night when we celebrated his birthday. He turned 37 years old and all I could think of was that I wish that was us celebrating your birthday. Oh well, hopefully someday. In the meantime, you should have seen the moon last night. It was spectacular.

Facebook Post

Miss me?

I have missed Y'all a ton. I am ready to hit the road running again. But first, we have a huge celebration at the Ranch.

It has been 39 years of cattle drives…

Hank's 90th birthday and his 60th cattle drive.

That may not make sense now, but when I get all the pictures and stories posted it'll be clear.

In the meantime, here's a picture from this morning of the guests this week.

And the moon last night.

#epicRoadtrip

#epiclivingwithjean

#wontstop

Chapter 25
Idaho and Utah: Change of Plans

"Like the fish in the lake
And the cane pole you make
And the feeling when one's on the line.
Like the smile of a friend
Glad to see you again
That erases the passing of time.
Like the eagle that flies,
The sun in the sky,
Or the grace God has given to me
It's free, things I wouldn't trade for anything"

"Free"
Recorded by Jack Ingram

Writers: Jay C. Knowles and Trent Summar

Day 26: Sunday, August 22

I am a little frustrated. I should have been better prepared. I am heading out today but didn't check out the church situation when I was in town earlier and now, I am missing Mass. I have so much to be thankful for that I hate that I won't make it, but that does happen occasionally. I won't go into the theological discussion about it, but it does hurt my heart to miss it.

I hit the road at 9:00 AM, and at the top of the hill, I stopped and turned around to get one more photo of the Battle Creek Ranch gate. Dan is getting a ride to the Bozeman airport with the other guests, so I set my GPS and hit the road.

A few hours in I pass a sign for Monida, Montana, Exit 0. It sounds like a cool place to stop, but since I wasn't hungry yet, I decided to go a bit farther. Turns out it was a good thing I didn't stop. When I looked it up online to see what I missed, I learned that it is a community off of Interstate 15 at the top of Monida Pass, and is situated on the Continental Divide at the Idaho state line. It has a permanent population of six. Cool.

The name is derived from the first three letters of Montana, and the first three letters of Idaho. There is a deep history there and it once was a bustling town for tourism and cattle. Also cool.

From 1898 to 1907, a train stopped here and passengers could then take a stagecoach from Monida to Yellowstone National Park. More than 12,000 people passed through the town in the summer of 1902. When the stage line went out of business in 1909 due to the growth of motor vehicles and the building of a new train station closer to the park, people just drifted away. There are no hotels, no gas stations, no restaurants. It isn't a ghost town but close. That could have been a problem if I was hungry or needed a bathroom. I still wish I would have stopped. Another thing to do NEXT time I am in the area.

Later, I stop at a rest area to use the bathroom and stretch. I sit for a minute. I watch nature. And people. I am content. And peaceful. There is another traveler lying in the grass taking a nap and I think that is a wonderful idea.

First though, I need to make some decisions. My plan was to stay in Salt Lake City tonight but when I look at the number of miles to get to Dallas, I decide to rethink that. Somewhere in the back of my mind, I get the idea to see if Bryce Canyon is on my route. I have no idea what exactly is there, but I had a friend who had visited there and I just knew that it was to be my next stop. I look for the closest town, and then look for a hotel, (I learned my lesson).

I find a hotel in Hatch Utah, just outside the canyon and call, but had to leave a message. When I get done, I realize I had been sitting there over an hour and now I don't have time to nap…but I have a plan and that motivates me.

I cross into Utah at 5:00 PM and get a call from my oldest son. We end up talking for two and a half hours and while I drive, I tell him about how beautiful the landscape is. As I get into the Salt Lake Valley, there are mountains on both sides. The towering Wasatch Mountains to the east and the Oquirrh Mountains to the west. That's another item on my list for the next trip, spending a few days in Salt Lake City. I know very little about the area but it is beautiful.

I start to panic a bit. When I left the message with the

hotel, I noticed that the office closes at 8:00 PM and it is approaching that time. I was relieved when I finally got a call from them. I told them I wouldn't be getting there until 10:00 PM and they told me not to worry. They put me in cabin #15 and the key was on the table inside. I should just fill out the envelope that is also there with my credit card info and drop it off in the box on the way out in the morning. Just like in South Dakota. This is totally foreign to me, but beautiful and I couldn't wait to see what my 'cabin' looked like.

Day 27: Monday, August 23

It was a fascinating drive into the canyon area last night. It is dark here, but the moon is bright, so you could get a feel for the size of the rocks around you but you couldn't actually see them.

My cabin was cuter than I could have even imagined. What a beautiful place. I hate that I will only be here for a couple of hours. Once again, I am adding to my To-Do list for the next trip.

I stayed up late last night trying to figure out the best plan. I have to be in Dallas Tuesday night, and it is 18 hours from here. Looking at information on Bryce Canyon, since I won't be doing any hiking, the best way to see the park is the one main road that runs north and south. Straight shot up and back, 18 miles each way.

Bryce Canyon is known for two unique geological formations. The hoodoos are tall, thin spires of rock that are created through the erosion of sedimentary rocks, and composed of colorful limestone, siltstone, and mudstone. The process of hoodoo formation involves a combination of frost weathering and erosion by water. During winter, water seeps into the cracks in the rocks, freezes, and expands, causing the rocks to break apart. Over time, this process, known as frost wedging, contributes to the creation of the distinctive hoodoos.

Bryce Canyon also features natural amphitheaters, which are large, bowl-shaped depressions in the landscape. The amphitheaters in Bryce Canyon are a result of the unique erosion patterns that have occurred over millions of years. The combined effects of frost weathering, stream erosion, and the gradual retreat of the cliffs have shaped the landscape into these stunning formations.

The most famous amphitheater in Bryce Canyon is the Bryce Amphitheater, which is home to a concentration of the park's most iconic hoodoos, including Thor's Hammer and the Queen's Garden.

Overall, the combination of hoodoos and amphitheaters in Bryce Canyon creates a visually stunning landscape that feels like the set of a sci-fi movie.

The park is renowned for its sunrise and sunset views. The changing angles of sunlight create vibrant colors on the rocks, making it a favorite among photographers and has got me excited to get up early.

I figured I would get to the park around sunrise, drive the road up and back. Poke around a bit. Take some videos and lots of photos and then be back on the road by 10:00 AM. Once again, I am happy when I have a plan.

The cool thing about plans is that they can change in an instant. Sometimes the greatest things happen when your plan gets shot to hell. That is what happened, but it didn't start out that way.

I made it to the park before the sun crested the mountains. I knew this day was going to be special just by the beauty driving to the park. It was like nothing I had seen before. There were several roadside stops with information tables but I restrained myself, remembering that I was on a schedule.

Entering the park, I was greeted by a group of mule deer just leisurely eating by the side of the road, not at all concerned that I was interfering with their breakfast. It wasn't more than a mile up the road where I started to see beautiful views just through the trees on my left. I pull off onto one of the scenic loops and get out. There I see nature as I have never seen it before. I don't stop long, I need to keep moving.

A little farther up I pull off again. Then again. Finally, I realized doing it this way was taking too long, so I decide to drive up to the very top and work my way down.

The road ends at Rainbow Point. It was Rainbow Point where everything started new for me.

There were several groups of people there when I pulled in and parked. I waited until they all moved on to walk out to the viewing area. I had a feeling that this was the place I needed to be, and the moment I needed to be here. It wasn't that I didn't want to share it with anyone, but I was worried about falling apart in front of a bunch of people.

Rainbow Point is situated at the southernmost tip of Bryce Canyon National Park, and it stands as the pinnacle of the park's scenic wonders. This high-elevation viewpoint provides an awe-inspiring panoramic vista that extends for miles across the vibrant and colorful landscape of the Paunsaugunt Plateau. At an elevation of over 9,100 feet, Rainbow Point offers an unobstructed view of the amphitheaters and the intricate network of hoodoos that define Bryce Canyon. The name "Rainbow Point" is fitting, as the ever-changing hues of the rock formations, ranging from reds and oranges to pinks and purples, create a kaleidoscopic display.

From this vantage point, you can see all the geological intricacies of the park while marveling at the vastness of the surrounding terrain. It is not only a perfect spot for capturing the grandeur of Bryce Canyon but also for contemplating the forces of nature that sculpted this remarkable and unique landscape over millions of years.

Facebook Post

There are times that I am stunned by the beauty of our country.

This is one of those times.

#epicView

#epicRoadtrip

#epiclivingwithjean

#WontStop

I have no words to describe what happened when I walked to the edge and looked out. I could see for miles and miles. I felt an overwhelming sense of being on top of the world as if God conspired to create this masterpiece exclusively for me. I could feel His presence as never before.

I felt this was a symbolic beginning, a moment suspended in time when the world below seemed to fade away, and the expansive beauty of Bryce Canyon became a canvas painted by God, where he stepped back and said "You also are my creation, and this canyon does not hold a candle to the beauty and intricacy of you".

That moment had a deep personal and emotional significance. I felt a profound sense of awe and connection with nature and time.

As the sun moved in the sky, the hues of the hoodoos, changed as if dancing in the light. Little details that couldn't be seen one moment were jumping out at me the next. This ever-changing scene seemed to mimic my life and my journey. The forces of nature, though seemingly destructive, were what carved this canyon and created its beauty. Without those forces, the canyon would not be what is. What is meant to be.

Those are the same forces that I have been battling in my life for years. Relationships, health, expectations, disappointments, struggles, death. Each adding its own layer of carving out who I am to be. Who God created me to be.

I have found peace on this trip, but today was different. I found connection, purpose. An understanding of why I am here and a deep conviction that I am to surrender and let God work in my life.

In 1998 and 1999, there was a time when both my parents were battling cancer. They had always been a strong couple and did most everything together, but I told them that dual chemo treatments was going a bit far.

During that time, I drove back and forth from Virginia to Texas, probably 8 times. I would go down and spend a few weeks getting doctor's appointments, helping pay bills and getting treatments lined up, spending as much time as I could with them both.

It was a special time that I am so glad I had, but with each trip, it became harder and harder to leave. It got to the point that I would put the kids in the car and leave in the early morning hours because I couldn't bear having to tell them goodbye, in fear that that would be the last time that I would say it to them.

One morning, about an hour into the trip, at 5:00 AM, on some back road in Texas, I took off my watch and told God that I could no longer handle balancing everything that was happening. I gave Him control and said "If there is a place I need to be, You need to make sure I get there. If there is something I need to do, You need to make sure I see it, and if there is something I need to say, You need to give me the words". I promised that I would show up 100% and I would be open to whatever I was told to do. From that day I have not worn a watch, reminding myself that it is all in God's time.

That worked great for a lot of years, but sitting on top of that canyon, I realized how much I had backtracked. I was continually trying to anticipate problems, running interference, trying to understand other people's words and actions and making assumptions about everything. Then taking all the blame for everything and everyone.

Now, don't get me wrong, I don't believe that any of those things are inherently bad. As a mother, a lot of that list is important just to make things happen. BUT the moment that you lose yourself, your sanity, your peace of mind trying to juggle everything, it becomes a problem. A really big problem.

I knew, deep in my soul, that the health and emotional

struggles I was battling all stemmed from the stress of having to live up to the role I had created for myself. I was miserable, but it was me who locked the chains that I was dragging around.

All the conversations with Thumper started me remembering who I had been. Looking out over the canyon I saw who I was supposed to be. Who God created me to be. And what life was supposed to look and feel like.

I am not sure how long I sat there, but when I got my bearings back, I was ready to move.

As I was walking back to my car a man approached me and said he saw my license plates were from Virginia and asked where I was from.

"A little town outside of Richmond", my standard answer.

"Oh really? What town?" he asked.

"Powhatan, you have probably never heard of it."

"Actually, I am from Midlothian, Virginia," he replied.

For those of you who don't know, Midlothian is the town right next to Powhatan. He lived 20 miles from me. It is certainly a small world. He was on a road trip also, and so we compared travel notes, places we had been and places we wanted to see. We took a quick photo and I hopped in my car.

I may have experienced a monumental life-changing moment, but I still had a schedule to keep, so it was back down the Canyon road for me. After seeing the view from the top, I knew exactly where I wanted to stop on the way back down.

Black Birch Canyon, Elevation 8750

Agua Canyon, Elevation 8800

Natural Bridge, Elevation 8627

Bryce Pointe, Elevation 8300.

I was happy to see that the park was very accessible. I was feeling much better, but I would still get winded fairly easily and having paved walkways to the viewing areas made each stop manageable.

The viewing area at Bryce Point is the most iconic of the park's viewpoints. You turn off the main road at mile marker three then drive two miles on a spur road. It provides a soaring view of the Bryce Amphitheater from the south.

Southern Paiutes, a tribe of Native Americans who have lived in the Colorado River basin of southern Nevada, northern Arizona, and southern Utah call this place **Unka Tumpi Wun-nux Tungwatsini Xoopakichu Anax**, which means "Red Rock Standing Like a Man in a Hole". (by the way, I had to check my spelling of that several times, I was sure I wrote it down wrong)

These amphitheaters contain the world's greatest concentration of hoodoos. There is a Southern Paiute word for "scary" or "spirit" pronounced "oo'doo", which has been associated with this place. A sacred oral tradition of the Southern Paiute states that these hoodoos are ancient "Legend People" turned into stone by the trickster god Coyote as a punishment for bad deeds.

Another cool find, mounted in the ground on the walkway out to the viewing area is a marker that reads, "US Geological Survey Marker".

My plan was to be on the road at 10:00 AM and it is now after noon. I have some time to make up but it was worth every minute.

> *Make sure that you take a moment to check out all the photos and resources on my website. Scan the barcode at the beginning of the book and it will take you there. All the photos and resources are divided by chapter so they are easy to find.

Chapter 26

Arizona and New Mexico

"Baby we were born to run"

"Born To Run"
Recorded by Bruce Springsteen

Writer: Bruce Springsteen

Still Day 27: Monday, August 23

Back on the road and flying. I need to get as far into New Mexico as possible. There are so many cool places that I am driving by. I have to keep telling myself "NO".

The land here is beautiful. The rocks are changing from red to white. There isn't a lot of traffic, and there is a lot of space between towns. And actually, I wouldn't even call them towns. Just gas station/convenience stores on the side of the road. It is hot, but I am making good time.

Until I miss my turn.

Now, to be fair, missing my turn itself wasn't the problem. I realized it immediately and turned around the first chance I could. The problem arose when I noticed that the place I was turning around in was the entrance to Horseshoe Bend. When I saw the picture on the entrance sign, I knew I had to stop.

I drove up to the gate and told the attendant I missed my turn and just needed to turn around, but was interested in the sign. She handed me a flier and explained that Horseshoe Bend was a National Recreation Area and was one of the most photographed spots in Northern Arizona. That sparked my interest. I asked her how far the walk was to the viewing area. She told me not to worry, it was only a mile and a half round trip hike, and the walkway was paved with covered benches along the route to rest.

That was all I needed to hear. I paid my entry fee, parked and put on my hiking shoes. Mile and half? No problem. I can do this and be back on the road in no time.

Horseshoe Bend is a stunning natural formation located in Arizona, near the town of Page. Carved by the Colorado

River, this horseshoe-shaped meander offers breathtaking panoramic views of the surrounding red sandstone cliffs and the emerald-green waters below. The overlook stands approximately 1,000 feet above the river, providing visitors with a mesmerizing perspective of the winding canyon. Horseshoe Bend was mostly a local attraction until the growth of social media had people posting photos of the unique place. It is now a popular destination for nature enthusiasts and photographers, and people like me looking for cool spots.

I was in a hurry, not only because I was excited about this new adventure, and a chance to get out of the car and move for a bit, but I still had a long drive. I wanted to just walk up, get some photos and get back in the car.

The walk was paved and there was a pretty decent crowd for the afternoon.

1:52 PM, sent a text and a photo to my husband, put on my walking shoes and hit the trail.

2:06 PM, the walk to the rim was tougher than I expected, I had to push myself but the view was worth every step. It is pretty hot. I wish I thought to bring water with me. No worries, I took some photos and watched some kids climb up on the rocks.

2:10 PM Wished there was a bench at the viewing platform to sit, but I really needed to keep moving, so I start heading back to the parking area.

2:28 PM Had to stop and sit at the first bench. Thankful that there is some shade. Really wishing I had water now. Eyeing a Mexican family with a huge canister of water. Wondering if I remember the Spanish word for water.

2:40 PM I had to stop again. Shade. Rest. I am struggling bad now. Dehydrated, hot, a little delirious. I pretend I am doing something on my phone so people don't think I am about to pass out, BUT I am about to pass out. This is the first time since Indiana I have had issues with my heart and I wonder if there are some emergency people at the gate who can come get me. I send a message to Dan and tell him I am struggling and to send me a prayer.

3:15 PM I finally make it back to the parking lot. I have never been so happy to see my car in all my life. I was saved by a couple who had passed me on their way down and was passing me again on their way back.

They stopped me and asked if I was ok, I am not sure what I said. They did give me some water which helped a lot, and walked with me the last bit of the trail chatting with each other and with me, but I know I didn't say anything but thank you when we got to the top.

The ironic moment of the day. I noticed the sign that I was leaning on to catch my breath at the top…said, in bold letters..."Make sure you bring water."

Duh. Not my finest moment.

3:24 PM. Back on the road. Called Dan and told him I survived. Noticed that the temperature outside was now 99 degrees. No wonder I was struggling. I had also been up since 6:00 AM after not much sleep the night before. And on top of that, I had done a bit of walking already that day.

I took a selfie. Just to remind me that I CAN still do hard things. It just makes more sense not to put myself in that position. Hopefully, that photo will remind me of that too.

Still Day 27: Monday, August 23

Back in my car and flying once again. This part of Arizona is home to the Navajo Nation, the largest federally recognized tribe in the United States. It extends into the states of Utah, Arizona and New Mexico, covering over 27,000 square miles of unmatched beauty. Diné Bikéyah, or Navajoland, is larger than 10 of the 50 states in America.

Today, the Navajo Nation is striving to sustain a viable economy for an ever-increasing population that has now reached over 250,000. In years past, Navajoland often appeared to be little more than a desolate section of the Southwest, but it was only a matter of time before the Navajo Nation became known as a wealthy nation in a world of its own. The discovery of oil on Navajoland in the early 1920s promoted the need for a more systematic form of government.

In 1923, a tribal government was established to help meet the increasing desires of American oil companies to lease land for exploration. The Navajo government has evolved into the largest and most sophisticated form of American Indian government and hosts 88 council delegates representing 110 Navajo Nation chapters.

While the Council is in session, you'll likely hear delegates carry on the tradition of speaking in Navajo, providing a perfect example of how the Navajo Nation retains its valuable cultural heritage while forging ahead in a modern world.

In WWII the Navajo language was used to create a secret code to battle the Japanese. Navajo men were selected to create codes and serve on the front line to overcome and deceive those on the other side of the battlefield. These men were recognized as the Navajo Code Talkers, who exemplify the unequaled bravery and patriotism of the Navajo people

The land is barren and beautiful. No towns, but occasionally there will be a ranch or business. I am very conscious of my gas tank because stations are few and far between, and if I were to get stranded, there is nowhere to walk to.

Facebook Post

Jean Tillery is in Shonto, AZ.

Flying through this beautiful country listening to Cliff Cody

It is 6:45 PM and I just passed a sign that reads "Many Farms Chapter House."

Many Farms, or Dá'ák'eh Halani, as the local members call it, began in 1937 as a small farming community near an irrigation dam, 15 miles North of Chinle, Arizona. Early on the town came to include a few clusters of residential homes. During World War II, the people of Many Farms raised and harvested livestock.

In 1941, Many Farms became the site of the Navajo Tribal Slaughter House and Cannery, which supplied fresh and canned meat from local livestock for schools and hospitals on the reservation. In fact, they packed and shipped livestock products to the armed forces.

Today, Many Farms is identified as a secondary growth center with educational and community facilities, public governmental services (tribal, county, and state), commercial businesses, and the traditional livelihood of farming and ranching. It resembles other small desert towns scattered throughout the west.

As I drive through this land there are two things that stick out to me.

First, almost every property I pass has a round, wooden circular building on it. I learned that they are known as "hogans." Hogans are traditional dwellings that hold deep cultural and spiritual significance for the Navajo people. These structures are typically made of logs and earth and have a distinctive, circular design.

There are two main types of hogans: the "male" or "grandfather" hogan and the "female" or "grandmother" hogan. The male hogan is typically larger and used for ceremonial purposes, while the female hogan is smaller and serves as a more everyday living space.

Hogans are not just homes; they are considered sacred spaces where various ceremonies, rituals, and traditional activities take place. The construction of a hogan involves specific cultural practices, and the orientation of the structure is often aligned with astronomical and spiritual considerations.

While modern housing has become more prevalent, hogans continue to hold cultural importance, and many Navajo families maintain them on their properties as a connection to their heritage and a place for cultural practices.

The second is that there are a lot of signs at the entrances to properties that say "Absolutely no visitors" and "Stay home"

It seems that COVID has struck the Navajo population

hard, and even now, they are trying to protect their families as it is common to see several generations of members living together.

I cross into New Mexico at 8:00 PM. It has been a long day, but I am driving as far as I can. The more miles today, the closer to Dallas I will be for tomorrow.

Chapter 27

I Woke Up This Morning With Texas On My Mind

**"I woke up this morning
Texas on my mind"**

"Texas On My Mind"
Recorded by Pat Green

Writer: Django Walker

Day 28: Tuesday, August 24

Facebook Post

in Grants, NM.

Good Morning!!

I'm exhausted but I'm out the door.

10 more hours to Dallas!

My favorite day will always be the day I wake up knowing I am heading to Texas. I haven't lived there in a long time, but it will always be home for me. I am lucky that with all the family, friends and Texas music, I am back often.

This trip has me heading to Dallas for the eWomenNetwork ICON Conference. I am in a time crunch, but I do plan on heading to College Station after the conference to see some old friends. I always hate when I can't spend a lot of time in Texas, there are so many people I want to see, so many things I wish I could do. It is stressful having to pick and choose, but I need to be in Oklahoma next Monday and back in Virginia by the end of next week. I am really thinking that I need a little Robert Earl Keen in my life. He has a song with the line "The Road Goes on Forever"...this is the point that I wished it did.

I cross into Texas at 11:00 AM.

Facebook Post

Jean Tillery

My favorite sign!

Cue my Texas Playlist…

I pull up all my favorites as I cruise through my home state.

The majority of the music I listen to is described as Red Dirt Music and/or Texas Music. The two share similarities and are often considered part of the broader Americana music genre. Both have strong ties to country, folk, rock, and blues. While Red Dirt Music originated in Oklahoma, Texas Music has its roots in, obviously, the state of Texas.

Texas Music encompasses a diverse range of styles, including country, outlaw country, folk, and rock. Artists like Willie Nelson, Waylon Jennings, and Townes Van Zandt have played significant roles in shaping the Texas Music scene. Over time, Texas Music has evolved to include a wide array of musical expressions, reflecting the rich culture of the state.

The connection between Red Dirt Music and Texas Music lies in their shared influences, a focus on songwriting, and a commitment to being authentic, and having a grassroots approach to the music and the music industry. AND touring heavily and creating a dedicated fan base.

Musicians from both genres often collaborate, perform in similar venues, and participate in festivals that celebrate the broader roots music community, like my favorite music festival, Mile 0 Fest.

I always try my best to hit at least one live show every trip and this one is no exception. I snag a ticket to see Roger Creager who is playing in Plano Texas about 30 minutes north of me on Thursday night. It will be a great break from the conference.

Facebook Post
August 24, 2021

Jean Tillery is in Jolly, TX.

I just had to check in from here.

What a great place to live

I don't think I have ever driven into Texas from the west. I am passing through small town after small town. Rural farming towns, many are suffering the same thing as small towns all over the US, empty buildings, closed stores, dwindling populations.

The reasons are mainly the same, economic challenges, aging population, limited educational and healthcare facilities, rural-urban migration for example. It is sad for me to see as I love my small town back in Virginia.

And that stands in stark contrast to the view pulling into Dallas.

Chapter 28
eWN: Lift Others
As We Climb

"We are family
I got all my sisters with me"

"We Are Family"
Recorded by Sister Sledge

Writers: Bernard Edwards and Nile Rogers

Day 29: Wednesday, August 25

I am a member of a women's business organization called eWomenNetwork. It is a global community of women business owners, and entrepreneurs led by CEO Sandra Yancey. Every summer they host an International Conference (ICON) in Dallas for women (and men) who are passionate about their business and are ready to take their success to the next level.

I first attended an ICON event in 2018 when I was the Managing Director of the eWN Chapter in Richmond Virginia. Although I am no longer the MD, I still experience the value of the organization and the people that I have met there. They are my tribe, and I have become close with many of my "sisters".

This morning found me up early. I was meeting the Managing Director of the Northern Virginia chapter and we were going to walk before everything got started. The pre-conference events start at 9:00 AM and after a long day in the car yesterday, I needed to move.

I was excited about the week; this event provides so much inspiration and so many opportunities for collaboration that I want to be at my best so that I can take in everything.

There is only one thing holding me back.

I have had a disturbing feeling welling up in me. It started yesterday, about the time I crossed into Texas. I still hadn't heard anything else from Thumper, and although I have sent a few messages over the last few days, like the others, they were not received. I am not sure where this feeling was coming from, but by lunchtime, I was in a panic. I was sure that something had happened to him, sure that something was wrong. I didn't know what, or how, but I felt that him reaching out to me was causing him some type of distress.

After lunch, I went back to my hotel room and still wasn't able to calm down. So I did the only thing I thought I could do.

I sent a message to Thumper's fiancé.

Text Message
2:33 PM

"Please don't delete this, please read it.

I saw that you unfriended me on Facebook and know you were trying to put some distance between us and I promise I will respect that after I send this text.

I know Thumper is trying to distance me too. It is not a surprise...this is a very strange situation and I've been fine with that up to now.

For some reason in the last 12 hours I have had this overwhelming dread feeling about him and I am so scared that something is wrong and just have to know that he is ok.

You guys reached out to me and it changed everything for me in such wonderful ways. I really wanted a chance to get to know him and you and your families and I hope that someday that will still happen. But for now, I'll just settle for knowing he is ok.

I do want to thank you so much for finding me. I will never be able to pay you back for what you've given me. But I do promise going forward I will not reach out to you again unless you do it first."

Reply:

"Do not text me again, it is not your concern what is going on with him one way or another and neither of us want anything to do with you. You will be blocked from my phone after this message."

I read her response. Over and over. Five minutes. Ten. Finally, in my best Scarlett O'Hara accent, I thought to myself…"I can't think about that right now, if I do, I'll go crazy. I will think about it tomorrow."

Then I headed back downstairs.

Day 30: Thursday, August 26

I skipped the morning session today because I had set up a photo shoot with an eWomenNetwork sister. She is an amazing photographer, and during the conference, she will set up a 'booth' and do mini-sessions. I had reached out to her months ago about doing a session with her as I would need a photo for the book. I asked her if I could bring some 'props' for the shoot and she eagerly said "yes".

This was the first time I got to work with her and she giggled when I showed up with a box of cool props, all related to my #epicRoadtrip. I had a blast! She has an amazing ability to make even the most nervous person feel at ease in front of her camera and manages to capture your unique beauty in a wonderful way. The mini-session was no more than ten minutes, but she managed to get some really great photos.

Facebook Post

Epic Living with Jean is at Embassy Suites by Hilton Dallas Frisco Hotel Convention Center.

Frisco, TX

Photoshoot for the #epicRoadtrip book that will be coming out based on the AMAZING trip! The fabulous @turpenoffphotography made me feel fabulous and got so many great shots...in only 10 minutes.

#epiclivingwithjean

#epicRoadtrip

#smileforthecamera

The afternoon conference sessions are over and I feel like my head will explode. Sandra and her team, husband Kym, and daughter Briana work together, tag teaming the teaching, each with their own area of expertise. Sandra is all about business...systems, procedures, numbers. Unlike a lot of conferences, I have attended, Sandra pours the information into you and shares her knowledge like no other person I know of. She is best at showing you how to stop thinking and acting like a 'business owner" and start thinking and acting like a CEO.

There is a difference and that difference is crucial to scale your business.

Kym is the President & CMO, and a marketing genius. It is also a plus in my book that he is a Former Capitol Records, Gold-Record Winning composer and producer who's won over 200 awards in advertising.

Briana Dai, the Creative Director, has an eye for design and a knack for social media and branding. I was able to work one-on-one with her when I developed the new branding for my Epic Living with Jean company. She is as brilliant and beautiful as her mom and started her career in makeup and beauty so she is a treasure trove of knowledge in that area as well.

The genius of what these three have built at eWomenNetwork is that there is a whole "Success" system. No matter what stage your business is in, you move through the programs as you scale to the next level, and then the next.

Sandra's mission with eWomenNetwork is to have one million women, each having one million dollars in annual revenue. It is MY mission to be one of her "made it to a million" recipients by 2030.

(Check out the resources section of my website to learn more about eWomenNetwork and reach out to me if you have any questions)

Facebook Post

Epic Living with Jean is at Embassy Suites by Hilton Dallas Frisco Hotel Convention Center.

Frisco, TX

It is time to increase my success, my results and my profits by serving in bigger and better ways

#IAmAnIcon

#ewnICON

#eWomenNetwork

#epicRoadtrip

#epiclivingwithjean

Still Day 30: Thursday, August 26

I think the best part of the last 24 hours is the number of friends that have seen me and told me how much better I look than when they saw me earlier in the year. Finally… people see the difference that I have been feeling for the last few weeks. I am having a blast catching up with old friends and meeting new ones. I met someone today who had never even been to an eWomenNetwork event, but was invited by a colleague and hopped on a plane for Dallas. I sat down and interviewed her for my podcast just because I wanted to hear what attracted her to this group. It is the same thing that most of the members will say. This is a no-competition zone. One of Sandra's sayings is we "lift as we climb". That is not just a saying, in fact, it is a part of our organization's nine core values. You can see it everywhere at the conference. Collaborations starting, friendships developing, we learn from each other, and we cheer for each other. It is like no other organization I have found. Which is good for me now. I am feeling great, I am active and engaged.

After the official program ends for the night I hang out for a while in the main ballroom. Several of the Speaker Network members are rehearsing on the big stage. Yes, eWomen has a program designed specifically for people who want to be speakers. I can only stay for a few minutes, but I get to see 2 of my favorite people do their 4-minute presentation.

That is another item on my dream list…to be a part of that program also and be able to get on stage and talk about the power of DREAMING. That is what I am thinking as I run upstairs to change clothes and grab my car keys.

It is much easier to keep my mind occupied and off of Thumper during the conference. There is so much to learn and so many people to network with that my mind stays busy. It isn't until I am back in my room that the realization hits me like a ton of bricks. The quiet has my mind racing. I keep hearing "neither of us want anything more to do with you." Over and over. That ending is so…abrupt and so permanent. I am still kind of in shock by it all.

I have the same problem tonight on my drive north to the city of Plano Texas. Roger Creager is playing at the Courtyard Theater there. I have always said that music heals, but it is not this evening. During the show, I am feeling off balance and having a hard time enjoying myself. The music isn't helping, singing along isn't helping either. There is only so much pushing aside the thoughts I can do before I just give up and find myself crying again. Good thing the place is dark and I am sitting off to the side alone.

Day 31: Friday, August 27

I wake up determined to get past last night. I hadn't had dinner; I hadn't had enough sleep and I was exhausted from so much "people-ing". I should know that is a combination for failure for me. When I need to do battle with my overacting brain I need to be at my best.

I spend some time manning the podcast booth. I am a part of that program through eWomenNetwork and the booth gives me a chance to meet people who are interested in getting their stories out and it is giving me a chance to find my next interviews.

Friday night, several of the chapters are going out for dinner as a group, and since I am the lone person from my chapter this year, I get several invitations to join, but I have other plans tonight. I have a friend that lives in Fort Worth and we are meeting at my favorite BBQ place.

I met David on one of our Montana Cattle drives and we have kept in touch all these years so I am heading to the Stockyards to meet him for an early dinner.

The Fort Worth Stockyards is a historic district that was a major center for the cattle industry in the late 19th and early 20th centuries. The stockyard area was established in 1866 as a hub for cattle ranchers and livestock traders. Ranchers would drive their cattle to Fort Worth because there was easy access to railways that would transport the cattle east where demand for meat was high.

There is a lot to do in the district, from the daily cattle drives where a group of "cowboys" drive a herd of longhorns down the Exchange Ave reenacting the Old West cattle drives, to the famed Billy Bob's Texas.

Known as the" World's Largest Honky Tonk" it is a country music venue offering live shows and dancing. There is also the Texas Cowboy Hall of Fame and a lot of places for shopping. Today though, I am heading to Coopers Old Time Bar-B-Que. My favorite place for Texas brisket.

The original Coopers was opened in 1962 in Llano, Texas, that is still my favorite one to visit, but there are now 5 locations around Texas including the one in Fort Worth. Cooper's is a legendary Texas barbecue joint that offers high-quality meats cooked using a unique cowboy-style pit barbecuing technique over mesquite coals. There is nothing better than the thrill of walking right up to the pits and choosing what you want for your meal. For me, brisket is always the number one choice.

No one does brisket like Texas does, and people will argue for weeks about who has the best, and for me, it is always Cooper's. Just one of the many things my husband and I disagree on.

David let's me interview him for my podcast. He has lived a great story and we have a lot of laughs while he shares it.

As we are packing up to leave, he tells me that I need to go check out the area where the crew from "Yellowstone: 1883" has made over a couple of blocks into a film set. Normally, that would have been something I would have loved to do, but this week has started wearing on me and at the moment I want nothing more than my bed.

Facebook Post

Jean Tillery is at Cooper's Old Time Pit Bar-B-Que Fort Worth.

August 27, 2021

Fort Worth, TX

I am in my BBQ happy place!

Thanks to old cowboy's friends.

Chapter 29
Wish We Could Go Back In Time

"Wish that we could go back in time
I'd be the one you thought you'd find"

Recorded by: Cam

Writers: Cam Ochs, Jeffery Bhasker and Samuel Tyler Johnson

Still Day 31: Friday, August 27

Sleep won't come. No matter what I try I can't stop thinking. I try to read, I write, I even turn the TV on, which is something I never do. I read and reread the text messages. I go back through every word. What happened? What did I say? Or not say?

I am mad. At myself. At God. I am disappointed. I am frustrated. I start to question everything. Rationally, I know that the chances of having any kind of relationship with Thumper were slim. The stories of reconciliations make great Hallmark movies but they are not the norm.

I ask myself the one question I have been ignoring since the day I got the last text from Thumper. Do I regret that he reached out to me? Would I be better off not knowing he was out there? Would I go back if I could?

Thumper and I talked about walls. The walls that we build to protect ourselves. I never realized how many walls I had built. The problem with the walls is they might seem like protection, but what they are really doing is cutting you off. Years of dealing with things by not dealing with things.

We only had a few days of talking together, but those conversations re-ignited a flame in me. I know that the changes that I have experienced the last few weeks needed to happen and I am not sure there was any other way that they would have. Would I go back? No. Never. I hated the person I had become and I didn't even know how I got there. I certainly didn't know how I was going to get out. I wasn't even sure there was an out.

But now I know there is another side. I have seen it.

I have felt it. I was there, sitting at the edge of the world and I saw the potential. I won't ever forget. I am, though, coming to the realization that this trip is just one step in what could be a long process of healing.

That realization doesn't really help me tonight. Even at an event with hundreds of people, many of whom I know, I am feeling very alone. I want there to be something that I can do to fix things, but there isn't anything. Even if there was, Thumper doesn't want it.

I need to get out of my head, so I reach out to a friend for advice. Kevin is one of those people that I may only see once or twice a year, and usually for a short time, but we have been friends for a long time.

Chapter 30

Change of Plans Again...

"You're the reason I'm still here
Am I the one you were sent to save?
You came upon me wave on wave."

"Wave On Wave"
Recorded by Pat Green

Writers: David Neuhauser, Justin Pollard and Pat Green

Day 32: Saturday, August 28

The Saturday of the conference is always the same basic schedule. Sandra finishes her teaching and then after lunch there is a special guest speaker. I was super excited that this year, Stedman Graham was the speaker and he was going to stay after the program and if you bought one of his books, he would autograph it for you.

If you don't recognize the name, Stedman is best known for being the long-term partner to Oprah Winfrey, but he is a top-notch businessman in his own right. He is a prominent American educator, author, businessman, and speaker, and is recognized for his work in the field of personal development and leadership. Which is what he was talking about today. His talk focused on the importance of developing a strong sense of self and purpose. He was a great storyteller and so much of what he said really resonated with me and what I teach my clients.

Facebook Post
Saturday, August 28

Epic Living with Jean is at eWomenNetwork Entrepreneur Conference & Expo - Embassy Suites Frisco Tx.

Last day of eWomenNetwork ICON conference...our keynote speaker Stedman Graham is my new hero...

11 pages of notes...laughs...tears and new motivation!!

#RiseEachTimeYouFall
#ewomennetwork
#IAmAnICON
#ewnicon

My plan was to stay and get a book and meet Stedman, then join a couple of my eWN sisters and talk about what our action items are when we get home from the conference. That is another thing I have learned from Sandra. Knowledge is great, but it doesn't do anything unless you put it into action. I always try to leave an event like this with one or two distinct items I will start doing immediately. In the morning I would go to Mass and then head to College Station Texas to spend the night with another Texas friend. My oldest was going to meet me in CS so we could all have dinner together Sunday night and then I would be heading to Oklahoma Monday morning.

Late last night I decided to change my plans.

My conversation with Kevin cleared things up a lot. Funny thing is, we are polar opposites in a lot of what we believe in, but I trust him completely and I know that no matter what, he will be 100% honest with me. He is one of the few people that I know that really doesn't care what other people think about him. He is dedicated and a hard worker but he won't take shit from anyone. He always finds a way to challenge the boundaries of what I believe and what is important to me, and he makes me laugh. He was the perfect person to talk to. And we did talk. For four hours. About everything. Probably the longest conversation we have ever had. When the conversation was over, I knew I needed to go back to the one place that always made things better. The ONE place that I could always go that builds me up and reminds me why I am working so hard at this game called life.

That special place? Front and center of whatever stage Pat Green is playing on. He is the reason I found this genre of music and found all the musicians and songwriters that I love. I found him just weeks after my mom died, and the first time I saw him perform live was when I drove some furniture of my mom's down to my older brother in South Texas. I was hooked that first show. Now, almost 19 years and over 100 shows later, Pat still gets me back on course. There are so many people, so many memories tied up to him and his music. AND it just so happens that he was playing in Richmond Texas, right outside of Houston tonight.

If I get on the road by 2:00 PM, I can meet up with Kevin for dinner (to thank him for the lifeline he threw me last night) and be at the show by the time Pat hits the stage.

Facebook Post
August 28, 2021

I have a surprise!

It's my trip, and I can adjust my schedule as I see fit.

So right now I'm crusin' and I bet you can't guess where I'm going. And of course, my Texas music playlist is turned way up

(If you know you better not give away my secret)

It feels good to be on the move again. The weather is beautiful and traffic is not bad. A mandatory stop at Buc-ees for gas and Beaver Nuggets.

Buc-ee's is a chain of country stores, gas stations and electric vehicle chargers created and owned by Arch "Beaver" Aplin III. It was founded in 1982 in Clute,

Texas. It is known for the massive size of its locations, its distinct product offerings (gifts galore), its food, (jerky, fudge, brisket sandwiches to name a few), and especially the ultra-clean bathrooms.

As of now, they have forty-seven stores in Alabama, Florida, Georgia, Kentucky, Missouri, South Carolina, Tennessee and Texas. If you ever get the chance to stop at one, take it. I promise it is worth it. You will see why they have such a dedicated customer base, and why stopping and getting a selfie with the Beaver out front is such a "thing".

After a quick Mexican dinner with Kevin, I make it to Scotty's Saloon in Richmond Texas with enough time to find a spot on the side of the stage and some crates to sit on and I am set, just as Pat takes the stage.

Parking was kind of a pain. The venue is kind of out there. I finally ended up in a field, hoping that I would be able to find my car when it's all over, but for now, I am one happy camper.

The place was outdoors and the setup was wonky and hard to get around. It was packed and after talking to one of the people near me, I was warned not to worry about getting a drink because the lines were taking about an hour and the bathrooms were trashed. I made it through with no drinks and no bathroom breaks. It was just what I needed. Unlike the show on Thursday, I was able to relax and just enjoy the music. And the people watching.

Facebook Post
August 28, 2021

Jean Tillery is with Pat Green and Christopher Alan.

Maureen Bednorz Nadolski...you win the prize for the closest guess.

I went from Richmond VA

To Richmond IN

An Ended up in Richmond TX!!!

Like I mentioned earlier, I have been a die-hard fan of Pat's for almost 20 years. It isn't just the music, though I do love his stuff.

It isn't just the people I meet at his shows who have become lifelong friends.

What it mostly is…is Pat himself. For many years when we first started following him, Pat would make runs up the East Coast two times a year. I was homeschooling my kids at the time, so we could drive down to Charlotte, North Carolina and just follow him for a few nights.

We would hit up the museums and do school work during the day and then do Pat shows at night. My kids loved it. I loved it. But what was the most amazing was how Pat treated my kids. He would come over and talk to them whenever he saw them and was always available to sign stuff for them and take pictures with them. He was patient and kind with them. One night he even sat and watched my daughter do cartwheels down the beach after a show, making everyone else wait until my kids were done. I have a video of him talking to them from the stage at one of his shows. Those are the kind of memories that pop up when I see him, and that is why I keep showing up whenever I can.

Facebook Post

If there is a Pat Green show within a day's drive...I am there!

Here we go!

Facebook Post

Jean Tillery was live — at Scotty's Saloon.

Richmond, TX

Getting out of the place was a mess, but after the show, I was not going to let that bother me. As I waited for the crowd to thin, I went live on Facebook to tell a story. You can see the video on the resource page of my website, but the story goes like this.

Years ago, I had a dream that I was the star witness against an organized crime hitman and had to be put into the witness protection program.

It took only a few months for the bad guys to find me. When I asked them how they did it, they said they just staked out every Pat Green show until I showed up. Sounds about right.

Day 33: Sunday, August 29

I am back on the pre-conference schedule. Staying up late. Waking up early. Hitting the road.

After the show, I met my son at his apartment and stayed with him last night. We were up late talking; I hadn't really talked to him since our long conversation in Utah. It was great to catch up and I laughed when HE was the one who begged me to let him go to sleep.

Since I re-routed my trip through Houston, I got up

early and decided to do a bit of sightseeing before heading to Mass. I love to drive by my old schools, our old houses, places my mom worked, where friends lived. Our favorite hangouts.

I wonder if that is just a 'me' thing. I have so many ties to my life in Houston. So many wonderful memories there and I will always consider it home. I have been back to Texas often over the years, but I was always happy going back to Virginia. For the first time I ever remember, I am wondering why I haven't moved back here. All that has happened in the last few weeks has stirred up a lot of emotions and has me grasping for connection to something. I am not sure what it is other than I am really missing my parents. Somehow, seeing all these places makes me feel them. When I drove by the house my parents lived in after they left Indiana, I pulled over in the shade and pulled up directions to the church they used to attend so that I could go to Mass there. An elderly woman pulled out of her driveway and stopped next to my car and asked if I needed help. When I explained why I was there she was so sweet and kind. I don't remember what she said to me, but it brought me comfort. Which I was going to need. I am off to Mass, and the last time I was at this church was for my father's funeral.

Facebook Post

Jean Tillery is at St. Ignatius of Loyola Catholic Church.

Spring, TX

May I help you?

I have heard these words several times on this

trip. **Each time I truly needed something. Help, directions...a smile.**

Are you open to those that God puts in your path to help? They are all around us.

After Mass, I join my son for lunch, Mexican again? Of course! Afterward, I made a quick stop at my brother's house just to 'crash' his peaceful Sunday. It was a surprise because I hadn't originally planned to come to Houston. I had to laugh at everyone's shocked faces when they opened the door and saw me standing there. I didn't stay more than a few minutes because I was off to my last stop in Texas. My #epicRoadtrip was winding down and I had to get as much in as possible.

Facebook Post

Showing up at your brother's house And totally disrupting his

Sunday...priceless!

Too bad Dennis is so far away I would disrupt his day too!

Still Day 33: Sunday, August 29

It's a short drive to College Station Texas where I am staying with another longtime friend who I met at a Texas Music concert. The stay is short because of my Houston side-track, but he promised to give the grand tour after an early dinner.

College Station is the home of Texas A&M University, one of the largest and most prestigious universities in the state. It was founded in 1876 as the Agricultural and Mechanical College of Texas, the state's first higher learning institution. Like Purdue University, they were a land grant university and was established as a military institution. Although membership in the university's Corps of Cadets is no longer mandatory, they form the largest uniformed body of students outside of United States military academies.

Currently, they offer a wide range of undergraduate and graduate programs across various disciplines. They are best known for their business, agriculture, and engineering programs, and they also have one of the country's largest programs centered on recreation, parks, and tourism management.

All that information is great, but that is not what I am here to see. Growing up in Texas made me a football fan, and Kyle Field, the stadium at Texas A&M is the largest in the Southeastern Conference (SEC) and one of the largest in the nation. Named after Edwin Jackson Kyle, who was the Dean of Agriculture and the Athletic Council President of the university. It has a capacity of over 102,000 and even from standing outside it is a spectacular sight. I think I will have to add attending a game here to my Dream List.

Across the entrance to the stadium are the words "Home of the 12th Man". I asked what that meant, and was led to a bronze statue in the plaza with a plaque that read "On January 2, 1922, Texas A&M played Centre College in the Dixie Classic in Dallas. After numerous injuries to the Aggie team, coach Dana X. Bible called E. King Gill '24 from the stands. Gill, a basketball player and former football team member suited up. He never entered the game, but his willingness to support the team provided inspiration for victory. The strong support of Aggies for their teams keeps alive that special part of the Aggies spirit known as the 12th man tradition".

Since most football leagues allow a maximum of eleven players on the field at a time, referring to the Aggie fans as the "12th Man" implies that they have a significant role in the game.

As I read the plaque, I got a bit teary. That should be no surprise, it seems I cry all the time anymore…but I was moved by the idea of having a 12th man. I think we all need to have a 12th man. I vow at that moment to try to be that "man" for all those I can.

The students and alumni are nicknamed "the Aggies" because of the school's agricultural roots. They are known for their loyalty and respect to the university and its traditions. The 12th man is just one of the many that I learned about. I don't have space for it all, so check out my resource section on my website for more stories and links.

We finish the short tour with a stop at the famed "Dixie Chicken". Calling themselves the "oldest and most famous bar on Northgate" the Chicken was established in 1974 across the street from campus. It is 100% Texas with signs and photos and memorabilia covering every inch of the walls, and the wooden tables covered in names carved in the wood.

Two of my favorite Texas music icons have a tie to the Chicken. Robert Earl Keen and Lyle Lovett both attended Texas A&M and lived in a house behind the Chicken. They would often bring their guitars to the bar and hold impromptu concerts. If you listen to Robert Earl Keen's song "The Front Porch" he tells a story about that house.

Chapter 31
The Worst Thing About Texas

"The worst thing about Texas is having to leave"

"The Worst Thing About Texas"
Recorded by Lucas Jagneaux and the Roadshow

Writers: Lucas Jagneaux and Tobin Bruce Jagneaux

Day 34: Monday, August 30

Facebook Post

Happy Monday Y'all!

I love Mondays. Well maybe not THIS Monday, only because it starts off my final #epicRoadtrip days.

This has been a major, life-changing trip and although I miss Dan and Steve... I kind of don't want it to end.

In the meantime, I am leaving this message to you. Read it carefully and follow it to a 't'.

A Wish for the Week Ahead

May you listen more to your heart and less to the noise. May you attend to what is in front of you, and may you focus on what is in your control. May you remember that for every perfectly lit photo of a beautiful meal or scene of domestic bliss, someone is cursing and wondering why the floor is sticky. May you allow yourself to be sad, mad, weird, or whatever you need to be. May your coffee be hot, may your temper be cool, and may your WIFI be speedy.

Leaving College Station and starting the last leg of the trip. Working my way home doesn't seem to be as exciting as heading West at the start of the trip. The weather is beautiful and the sun is shining, so at least it is a great day to travel.

I was going over a conversation I had with my friends last night. From the moment I started this trip I have felt such a deep healing.

When I was in Kentucky at the "Ark Experience" I started the shift to offering every day to God to do with it what He wanted. Even with all the emotional ups and downs with Thumper and my health, I have been amazed at just how magical this trip has been. I have seen and said and done things I never would have dreamed I would do. I made the comment that I wasn't sure if this trip was an example of what my life would be like going forward, or if this was my swan song, my last notable accomplishment. Either way, I am glad I did it. I am glad that the opportunity presented itself and that I was able to pull it off.

I wonder how many other people get opportunities like these and pass them up? How many people let all the challenges and fears rob them of their potential? Over and over again while traveling and talking about my trip people would say, "I wish I could do that", "I could never do that", "I don't have time", "I don't have money", "My spouse, my children, my job, my responsibilities, will never let me do it". Did you see the movie "How to Lose a Guy In 10 Days"? The scene where they were playing cards at Matthew McConaughey's character's parent's house? Well, I call "Bullshit".

As a Dream Manager, I believe that our dreams are ours for a reason. They are given to us for a purpose we may never know. The dream of traveling across the country had been a dream of mine, written on my very first Dream List in 2010 and written over and over every year when I made a new list. It took me 11 years to make that Dream come true. There is no reason that any of those people could have made this trip. It may have taken THEM ten years. Or fifteen. Or maybe seven. I am no different than any one of them…other than the situations that happened in my life drove me to pursue this dream when I did.

Facebook Post

That post above is a line from a Josh Abbott song called "My Texas". I love the song because it is a list of fun things to do in Texas then proceeds to add, if you haven't done them…then you ain't met MY TEXAS yet.

The list is all pure Texas things. Things you probably wouldn't recognize if you weren't from Texas. I am proud to say that the list of twenty-four things…I have done all but seven. Look up the song. See if you can guess which seven I still have to do. Anyway…let's talk kolaches. It's really a thing. And in Texas, a BIG thing.

Brought to Central Texas in the late 19th century by Czech families, kolaches are a staple, especially in the small town of West, Texas, (not to be confused with the region of West Texas). There has always been a bit of confusion over the Czech definition and the Texas definition of what a kolache actually is.

Kolaches are pastries made of yeast dough and traditionally are fruit-filled, usually poppy seed, apricot, prune and a simple farmer's cheese. It is similar to what others would call a fruit Danish (but better).

Texans though, as they usually do, put a spin on them, and you will now find them with savory stuffings like sausage, eggs, cheese and jalapenos. Czech purists, though, will tell you that those are actually "klobasniky" and not kolaches.

I call them both delicious and the cool thing is, whether you are headed north on Interstate 35 or south, there is an exit with a Czech bakery right there for you to buy some. There are arguments over which bakery is better but as far as I am concerned, give me one, I don't care where it came from.

Still Day 34: Monday, August 30

Cross into Oklahoma at 6:34 PM. Not quite an hour until I make it to tonight's stop. Another friend...putting me up for the night. Hopefully, I can do laundry.

It was a little sad leaving Texas this time. The feeling that it was calling me to move back was strong. It was not even a week ago that I was pulling into Texas and searching Spotify for all the songs I could find about Texas. One of the songs that popped up was from Lucas Jagneaux and the Road Show. The song was titled "The Worst Thing About Texas" and when I read that, I was a bit out of sorts. I mean, really. There is no "worse thing about Texas". At all. Of course, when I actually listened to the song, I understood. "The worst thing about Texas is having to leave." That is very true today.

Chapter 32

Change of Plans
Once Again

"Should I stay or should I go?

"Should I Stay or Should I Go?"
Recorded by The Clash

Writers: Joe Strummer and Mick Jones

Day 35: Tuesday, August 31

I made it to Oklahoma. I got to my friend's house before she did, so I spent a few minutes on her deck with my feet in her pool and her dog's head in my lap. I am so enjoying the quiet. This trip has made me realize just how loud and noisy our lives are. The peace and the warm sun are lulling me to sleep. I am contemplating laying in one of her lounge chairs for a quick nap when she arrives.

She is another music friend and not only does she and her husband enjoy the same music as me but he is also a musician. I love that there are so many creative people in my life. AND I love to see the number of guitars he has. Makes me feel better about my stash of scrapbook supplies.

We caught up as we prepared dinner together. It was a really early night, but the laundry got done and loaded back in the car. I slept really, really good.

Which allowed me to get up and go early this morning.

One of the things that I have noticed during this trip, as I have shed my need to control everything and just let God lead me, I have found myself doing and saying things that would usually be way outside my comfort zone. Today for example. I am on my way to Tahlequah Oklahoma to meet up with the fabulous Amber Watson. Amber is a singer/songwriter/photographer/artist. I had bought a painting from her a while ago and on a whim asked her if I could interview her for my podcast.

I bribed her with lunch and we were meeting up at a local coffee shop to chat.

Still Day 35: Tuesday, August 31

Heading to Tennessee. The interview with Amber was amazing. We had so many laughs. She is not only smart and funny and talented (and beautiful) but she is open and honest and I was really moved by our conversation.

There was only one problem. We started the interview after we ordered our food. When they brought it to us, Amber paused the recording and then started it back when we were done eating. After we finished the interview, I drove around the cute little town of Tahlequah and took some pictures of the murals that Amber had painted on some of the local buildings. When I got back in the car and started to listen to the interview, the recording got hung up after 10 minutes. It said that there were 37 minutes of recording, but every time I tried to listen, it stopped at 10 minutes.

I was disappointed but surprisingly not upset. It was a wonderful interview, we talked about dreams and boys, and expectations. Who we are and who we want to be. I loved getting a chance to see that side of her. AND I guess that means we will have to meet up and do it again.

Facebook Post

I just crossed into Arkansas.

I think it is my state # 21.

But I'm not sure.

I'm not quite sure what day it is.

All I know is it's almost over.

And that kind of makes me sad.

As I drive, I am trying to decide what to do my last days. I have a friend in Nashville that I am talking to about meeting for breakfast, of course, a stop in Memphis to see Graceland is a consideration.

Facebook Post

Jean Tillery is at Fairfield Inn & Suites Memphis Germantown. Germantown, TN

Thank you, Danna, for the leftovers...they saved me tonight.

I am crashing for the night. I have a BIG day tomorrow.

Day 36: Wednesday, September 1

Well, my plans have changed once again. No stop in Nashville. I got a text message from my friend that I stayed with the other night. Both she and her husband tested positive for COVID so to keep everyone safe I am just heading home.

I am kind of bummed that the trip is ending this way. Of course, it is ending like it started. With no fanfare. I am sad I am missing my friend Ben.

I am just lying in bed playing on my phone, pouting. Trying to find a dopamine rush that will get me motivated to get on the road.

And I do find it...

Facebook Post

They say, begin with the end in mind.

Keeping that in mind. I just booked the entertainment for the launch party of the book from my #epicRoadtrip.

Looks like Courtney Patton will be visiting Powhatan VA in 2022.

Looks like I better start writing!

(PS...I love you Dan and it's always better to beg forgiveness than ask permission, right?)

Courtney Patton, another of my favorite singer/songwriters, is coming out with a new record, and in order to fund the project, she is offering to do house concerts and I just bought one. At least, my business did. I can't wait to have her play at my house. We haven't set a date yet, but it would be the perfect book release party.

11 hours from home, I won't make it today but I will go as far as I can and see where I end up.

Day 37: Thursday, September 2

Facebook Post

Have you been wondering where I am? Wondering if I decided to move into Graceland and eat peanut butter and banana sandwiches with Elvis's ghost?

Naw. Sadly, the story is much more boring than that.

Wednesday as I was getting ready to leave the hotel, I got a message that someone I was with earlier in the week had tested positive for Covid. I canceled the last two days of my trip to be respectful of people I might have contact with and just came home.

It was a very quiet return. Dan was gone and Steve was still mad that I left him for 5 1/2 weeks. My car is still loaded down, I am slowly working through all the stuff I accumulated...I have started writing...this book will be more than I ever imagined.

The good news is that I tested negative for Covid this morning...glad that I don't have to go through that again... and I have started writing. The book about the trip has taken off in a WHOLE new direction. It is not just a journal of a trip...it is a journal of a heart.

Now that I am putting the pieces together...I promise some pictures but first...since I am feeling better...I have a date with my rowing machine.

#epiclivingwithjean

#epicRoadtrip

#epicHome

#wontstop

Chapter 33
Home Sweet Home

"I'm going to Galleywinter

Place where all the cowboys ride

Place where all the outlaws hide

Away from the men who want to kill them for what they've done

I'm going to Galleywinter."

"Galleywinter"
Recorded by Pat Green

Writer: Pat Green

Still Day 37: Thursday, September 2

Years ago when I was designing my dream house I knew that it had to have a name. All the cool houses had names, especially in Virginia.

Monticello

Mount Vernon

Ashcroft Hall

Graceland

My husband, being the hunter he is, wanted to call it "Turkey-something or another" which I didn't want at all. We were debating the potential names as we drove to North Carolina for a Pat Green concert. Of course, we had a Pat CD playing as we drove, when his song Galleywinter came on. The song is about an imaginary place where Pat and his brother would play where "all the cowboys ride, place where all the outlaws hide away from the men who want to kill them for what they've done" We looked at each other and said "That's it" and from that day, our house was known as Galleywinter.

After all the years planning, and building, we did a lot of the work ourselves, it is a magical place for me. It is so good to be home.

It ends as quietly as it began.

No ticker tape parade.

No awards, no fans lined up for autographs.

I am tired but in a good way.

I feel different. Like I have seen behind the curtain of a magician's act and I now know how all the tricks are done.

Yet somehow that doesn't make me sad. It gives me strength.

I hadn't realized how much I had changed over the last 6 weeks. I hadn't realized how the walls I built that I thought were protecting me, were actually cutting me off from who I was, separating me from the people that I needed for support and love, and holding me back from true joy.

I don't have much time to think about it, as it is back to work and catching up on everything I missed.

Heading to California for a wedding.

Then to Dallas for a mastermind weekend.

Then my daughter's engagement party and wedding dress shopping.

Back to Texas in early October for a conference and two Jack Ingram shows at my favorite venue.

It is a very good thing that I am busy. I am finding it harder and harder to get back to that peaceful place. I find myself sad. Sad for missed opportunities. Worried that I did something wrong. Scared that somehow, I hurt Thumper or disrupted his life.

November has me back at CrossFit, just like I said I would be. Though this time I am working with a personal trainer who can come up with specific workouts for me working around my health issues. After a week I realized that one-hour sessions were too much and I cut them back to thirty-minute sessions. Then I cut them down to two times a week instead of three. Heading into the holidays even that is too much for me, but I am committed to finding a way to get healthy and be 100% me again. I remember what it is like to be that person and I want to be her again and I won't stop, I will try everything to get there.

Chapter 34
Closing

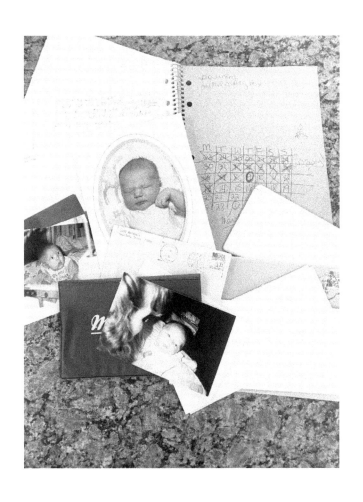

"When 1000 little pieces
Start Falling into place
It will show up right on time
However long it takes
When you just can't figure out where your supposed
to go
Love already knows"

"Love Already Knows"
Recorded by Ben Danaher

Writers Ben Danaher and Marti Dodson

A lot has happened since I got home. A lot hasn't happened.

I had to delete the 250+ text messages we sent each other. All the photos. His contact information. Once again, he lives only in my memory. The pictures, old letters from his adopted mom, journals, and all the things I wrote that he will never see are all back in a box.

When he first reached out to me it was kind of strange. When I think of him, he is a baby and I am 19 years old. It was amazing just learning about who he was as an adult. What he thought. How he felt. Who he loved. Who loved him. I told him it was the best entertainment I had, and that was the truth. I really enjoyed talking to him, he was smart and funny.

I was really happy. Really content. No expectations. I have had enough experience with this type of situation to know that the odds were against us. I even said to him that there were a million ways that this could blow up in our faces…

Our conversations brought back so many memories, so many feelings. Not all of them good, but all of them important. Who I was…what I believed. Where I came from, my family and friends, we touched on it all in that very short time. The wonderful part of having these conversations was that I was able to connect again with who I am. The person that had gotten lost years before. The person that I knew was gone but I didn't know where she went, or how to find her. Those conversations were the catalyst that gave me the ability to tear down six-plus years of walls that I had built. For the first time in a long time, I felt hope. And excitement. Freedom. Opportunity. Future.

And then I did it. What I told myself I WASN'T going

to do. Somewhere behind those walls was that memory of that last moment I held him. Somewhere in his words, questions, or smile, I found that piece of my heart I left with him all those years ago. And I fell.

Fell hard. I remember exactly when I realized what happened. I was sitting at a stop light in Chicago on my way out of town. Heading to Wisconsin. I knew it was too late. I knew I had gone too far. I knew I couldn't go back. And somehow, I knew it was going to end and I knew it was going to hurt. And it did. And it does.

The irony is that this is the same ache I had thirty-nine years ago. Back when I left for my first semester of college. Pregnant. Scared. I felt alone. I felt forgotten. I felt lost. Back then he was the one I connected with. He was always with me. I spoke to him; I sang to him. I carried him, I loved him and then I left him.

I can still feel him. I can still see his tiny fingers. I remember. I had never seen a baby that close up before and I was in awe. I remember looking in his eyes…telling him everything he needed to know. Telling him I would always love him and that part of me would always be with him and that all he needed to do was reach out for me and I would be there. And then I left him.

For weeks I would touch my stomach to feel him and then remember he was gone. I would still talk to him but there seemed to be an empty echo in my words. Time moved on. For a long time, I didn't. I existed in the world like an actor playing a role. Not sure who I was supposed to be and not sure what I could do with the empty hole in my soul.

But I soon got to work. I put my life back together and

went back to school. And I prayed. I prayed for the family that adopted him. I prayed for him to have loving brothers and sisters. I prayed that he would remember me. I prayed that somehow his soul would still hold a piece of my heart. I prayed to his guardian angel to keep him safe and well. I never prayed that he would look for me because I wanted his life to be so full of love that he wouldn't need me. I wanted him to think of me and thank me.

As time went on, I would wonder if he was happy. I would wonder if he had a dog…did he like to swim…did he love sports? The last contact I had from his mother was when he was nine. A one-page letter. One page could never give me all that I wanted…yet I knew that I had no right to more. The stories I read in that letter seemed almost foreign to me, but the picture…in that picture he was all mine. 9 years old but I could still see the baby I had once held.

Very few people in my life knew he existed…and I never ever talked about him. I was always scared that if I opened up I would end up giving away the last few tiny pieces I had of him and then he would be truly, totally gone.

I added this message to my growing stack of unsent letters in a box in my office.

To Thumper:

You asked me if I ever thought of you on your birthday. I found the box where I keep all my calendars and I checked…year after year Feb 9th is marked.

I also found some photos. Your first photo from the hospital along with the only pictures with the two of us together. They are old and faded and pretty worn.

My purse got stolen. The loss of cash and credit cards was a pain, but what broke my heart is that in a pocket of my wallet was a tiny silver cross from James Avery. My Godfather gave me two of them when you were born. One for me and one for you. I have carried yours around with me for 38 years and now it is gone.

I know you will never see this. I just wanted one more chance to say Happy Birthday to you, and thank you. Thank you for giving me my life back. Reminding me who I was.

The last few years have been tough. My physical healing needed to start with my spiritual and emotional healing and that all began with the first text you sent me.

Over the years I have reached out to many people for help, doctors, therapists, counselors, trainers, healers. I was desperate to become whole again, go back to who I was that day at Bryce Canyon when time stopped and my world was in perfect harmony.

I learned a technique called Ho'oponopono which is a Hawaiian practice of reconciliation and forgiveness that involves expressing remorse, asking for forgiveness, expressing gratitude, and expressing love in order to heal and transform relationships. It aims to bring about healing, understanding, and connection within oneself and with others...from me to you...

I am sorry

That you were put under stress and that I made things become difficult for you.

Please forgive me

For becoming so desperate about wanting a relationship with you and for putting you in the position that you had no other choice than to cut me out completely.

Thank you

For finding me and for reaching out. It is nice knowing that you are out there somewhere.

I love you

I have since the very first moment I learned you were there.

Chapter 35
Tying Up Loose Ends

"Hold fast, don't falter, take your troubles down to that alter and let it go.

Get going. Fear ain't a friend and I'm it's showing

You and me we've got more love then we could ever need

Let's share it baby.

Hold fast this was never meant to last."

"Hold Fast"
Recorded by Courtney Patton

Writer: Courtney Patton

When I planned this #epicRoadtrip it was going to be a huge launch for my Dream Manager Program. Fulfilling a Dream that had been on my list for years seemed like the perfect way to promote the program and give me a chance to step into my Crazy Dream Lady role.

This book was going to be strictly a travel journal. Information on the places I saw and things I did. I never imagined the upheaval that this trip would cause, but looking back I see it was all part of God's plan. He needed to give me something big enough to shake me out of the rut that I had dug for myself. He had to separate me from my routine and responsibilities. He put me in a car with hours and days to meditate and contemplate. He gave me a reason to look back through my life, the good times and the bad times, and remember that strong, determined girl that I had forgotten even existed. He gave me moments of pure peace and love, the kind of moments you only get when you completely surrender yourself and live intentionally and in awe.

He showed me that even though I may have lost that girl, lost that feeling, forgotten how to live that way…that I could get it back. He put me on the path, I just needed to start walking.

The trip was the first step but I have had to work hard to make progress. The journey was never easy. It was never just forward movement. I would get it together one moment only to fail miserably the next. Those moments may have taken minutes, or days or weeks. Overall, little by little, I started to heal.

It has taken me two years to finish this book. I have written and rewritten it again and again. Not that the story itself had changed, but my perspective of the story has changed. My ability to tell it has changed.

I feel like I am standing naked in the middle of a highway with everyone driving by looking at me. All my faults, all my mistakes, all my inadequacies on display. It may seem a bit masochist, and I am terrified of 'baring my soul'…but time and again I hear other women, and even men, tell similar stories and I hope that someone, even if it is just one person, finds hope, finds inspiration, finds strength from my story.

When I first sat down to start writing I asked myself, what do I want the readers to take away from my story? Other than the fact that I cry a lot.

I came up with four things.

1. **Trauma builds.** The undeniable truth is that life is hard. There are so many ways that we struggle and quite often we push those struggles away because we don't have time to deal with them. The problem lies when we continue to not deal with them. Each unprocessed difficulty left unattended, becomes a stone in the wall that blocks our mental and emotional well-being.

   There is a ton of research that supports the idea that unresolved trauma and chronic stress can have cumulative effects on both mental and physical health.

   Studies have shown that chronic stress can lead to a disruption of the stress response system, potentially causing conditions like anxiety, depression, and post-traumatic stress disorder (PTSD). Furthermore, long-term exposure to stress hormones like cortisol can have negative effects on various bodily functions, including the cardiovascular, digestive, and immune systems. I was the classic example of that.

I had a doctor tell me once that I was suffering from PTSD…and I laughed. No way, I said, that is what soldiers, first responders, and people who have extreme situations deal with. I wouldn't even call the things I went through trauma…I would call them "life". The doctor's response has stuck with me all these years. She said, "Your body does not know the difference". The chemical responses are the same. When you constantly live in a fight or flight state it will affect you dramatically.

I am not alone in this battle. Time and time again I meet and talk to women and men who struggle with the same things. COVID exacerbated the problem and we are seeing the fallout all across society.

2. **We can reclaim our lives.** Our mental and physical health may have taken a toll, but it is repairable. I spent years struggling with my health and doing everything the doctors told me to do. Nothing helped, and as I sunk deeper and deeper into frustration and despair, I became worse and worse. I was lucky that I was able to find a way to address, understand, and begin the process of overcoming the difficulties in my life. A lot of people don't have that opportunity. Or the opportunity presents itself but they don't see it for what it is.

This road trip gave me a chance to really work on

myself and start a process of healing. What will you do to jumpstart healing for yourself?

3. **I want to start a dialog around Adoption:** Let's talk about adoption. No sugar-coating, no beating around the bush. Adoption is a profound act of love—It is not an easy decision for either party, but I think we need to work on dispelling the misconceptions, the outdated stereotypes, and the judgmental whispers and bring it into the mainstream conversation. Adoption is a deliberate, courageous choice that deserves respect and understanding.

4. **The Dream Manager Program;** I have seen the power of dreaming firsthand, through my life, my friends, and my clients. I want to get everyone dreaming. All ages, all backgrounds, all walks of life.

   Do you have a big dream?

   Do you even have a small dream?

   Yours may not be to travel. Maybe going to college, buying a house, starting a business, having children. Maybe it's to get financially stable, learn a new language, volunteer at a food pantry.

Can you imagine the difference in our world if everyone took time to dream? Took time to figure out what amazing things they were created to do?

I can see that world. I believe we can get there.

In fact, I believe in it so much that I am starting a Million Dream Revolution.

Scan the QR code below for more information on how to join.

Chapter 36
FAQ About The #epicRoadtrip

"Still Good People, a lot of good people, still good people in this old world"

Recorded by Josh Grider

Written by Josh Grider

I already answered the question of why, but that was only one of the questions I get asked over and over. Here are a few more.

1. **Would you do it again?**

   In a heartbeat. There are so many places I missed and many that I would like to revisit. I am sure I will never be able to recapture the magic of that first trip though.

2. **What surprised you the most?**

   I was really surprised by how much time I drove in silence. I love music and had podcast episodes queued up, audiobooks, and even a stack of talks on CDs, but I still spent a majority of the time with my own thoughts. Dreaming, praying, or just listening to my heart.

3. **What was your favorite part about the trip?**

   The people. I met so many amazing people. At a time when the mainstream media was trying to divide us, I was reminded of all the good people out there. People were kind and respectful. The best of who we are.

4. **Weren't you scared?**

   I have to admit, there were a few times I was nervous. Like finding myself in a Walmart parking lot, late at night, somewhere in South Dakota, in a desperate search for a hotel room. For the most part though, I knew that with a AAA card, a cell phone, and a credit card, there was not much I couldn't handle. I tried to always be cautious and leave the rest to

God. I don't really think I was in any more danger on the road than I would be at home.

5. What was your biggest concern starting off?

My biggest concern in planning the trip was my health. I was in pretty bad shape.

Although this wasn't my first long trip, I wasn't sure that I would be able to pull 12 hours on the road like I used to. I worked closely with my health team to make sure that we had every scenario covered and a backup plan if I had to fly home part way through the trip.

6. What was your favorite place you saw or thing you did?

That is a really hard question. I tried to find really unique things to do, so considering that, I loved it all. Randyland in Pittsburg was one I would choose. It was so different and really appealed to my "hippy-chick" vibe. BUT my #1 favorite, can't wait to get back to, blow me out of the water surprise, was Bryce Canyon in Utah. It was a place not even on my original list, a last-minute side trip. It was almost painful in its beauty. I actually cried more than once just experiencing the glory. It was ever-changing as the sun moved across the sky. The light and shadows made it seem like a whole new place. I wish I could have spent all day there. I also wish I had the energy to actually do some hiking. I didn't do more than watch from the pull-off vistas and it still moved me beyond anything I have ever experienced.

7. How could you give up your child?

Yeah. I really had someone ask me that. It was a long time ago. Long before this trip. I was a part of an online program on adoption. They didn't know me. They didn't know my story. As with all virtual discussions, I had no idea of the tone of the question. They offered no more insight as to why they asked. I pray that it wasn't malicious, maybe it was a mother in the same position, or a child who had been adopted wondering what his/her birth parents went through. I am sure there are a few of you reading this with the same question in your mind.

I never say "I gave up my son". The truth is, I have never given him up. He is, and will always be a part of me. I placed him for adoption because I wanted him to have the best chance at a safe and full life with a family that adored him and loved him as much as I did. It was the hardest thing I have ever had to do. Even now, after him finding me, the hole is there.

We live in a culture that says everything, including life, is disposable. From the moment that I learned Thumper existed, I knew, no matter how inconvenient and painful it was, that this small baby had a purpose to fulfill in the world. A purpose that he was uniquely created to fulfill. I would give him life, but loved him enough to give him the best chance for a future.

8. Have you changed your feelings about your birth parents?

I will forever be grateful for my birth parents for choosing life, but I never felt like I didn't know who I was, or that there was something missing from my life. I grew up knowing that I was adopted and always felt that my adoptive parents were "my parents", and never really had any inclination to search for my birth family. I never blamed my being adopted for any of the bad choices I made in my life...or any of the good things either. I am who I am. That being said, there was a moment when I found the adopted.com website that I looked to see if I could find information about my birth family. Having no health history had never been a concern for me until I started getting sick and not knowing why. I did do a 23 and me DNA test for my nutritionist and if someone popped up as a close relative, I am sure I would at least communicate with them if they wanted.

Chapter 37
Resources

"I've been everywhere, man
I've been everywhere, man
Crossed the deserts bare, man
I've breathed the mountain air, man
Of travel I've had my share, man
I've been everywhere"

"I've Been Everywhere"
Recorded by Johnny Cash

Writer: Geoff Mack

Resources by Chapter:

There were so many places and so many people involved in this trip that there is not enough room to list them here. Find a complete list of places I went with links and information on my website by scanning the QR code below.

Photos:

I took over 8000 photos altogether while on this trip. I have narrowed that number down to the most important ones and have also posted them on my website. Please check them out.

Sponsors:

Also on my website are information and links for my trip sponsors. It was their belief in me along with their financial support that made this trip possible. I would love for you to learn more about them.

You can also find a list of all those who helped me in some way or another on this trip. From places to stay, meals, conversations, and donations, the support made my trip even more memorable.

Thank you!

Chapter 38
Find Me

"Come and Find Me Now"

Recorded by Josh Ritter

Writer: Joshua Ritter

This is my story, but everyone has their own.
I would love to know yours.

Reach out to me at jean@epiclivingwithjean.com

And follow me:
Facebook:
https://www.facebook.com/jean.tillery.1/
or
https://www.facebook.com/epiclivingwithjean/

Instagram:
https://www.instagram.com/epiclivingwithjean/

Website:
www.epiclivingwithjean.com

LinkedIn:
https://www.linkedin.com/in/jeantillery/

Pinterest:
https://www.pinterest.com/epiclivingwithjean/

Chapter 39

The Rest of the Story

"My feet are frozen on this middle ground
the water's warm here but the fire's gone out
I played it safe for so long, the passion left.
Turns out, safe is just another word for regret
So, I step to the edge and I take a deep breath.
We're all dying to live but we're all scared to death
And this is the part where my head tells my heart
you should turn back around
But there's no turning back now
I'm going all in
Head first to the deep end
I hear You calling
And this time the fear won't win
I'm going, I'm going all in
I'm all in, I'm all in
All in, I'm all in, I'm all in
I believe that one day I will see Your kingdom come
And I wanna hear You say,
"Welcome home My child, well done"

"All In"
Recorded by Matthew West

Writers: Pruis Andrew Jacob and Houser Jason C

It's November 2023.

Way past the first deadline I had to finish this book.

Way past the second.

And the third. Probably even thirty-ninth.

I never imagined it would take me so long to write this story. A lot has happened.

- I was robbed, my car was broken into while on vacation and I lost everything including the current handwritten manuscript of this book. I had to go back and re-write more than ½ of the work I had done.
- My health got worse.
- My daughter got married.
- My husband had a huge health incident and spent 32 days in ICU in South Carolina while I had to live in a hotel the entire time.
- I started getting better.
- Then I got worse again.

The entire time I kept searching for the way to get to that place I found on that trip. That place where I was completely in the moment. Completely being myself. Completely open to the immense possibilities and completely open and one with God.

I have been struggling with the understanding of "God's will" and have come to the following conclusions:

1. It's not my fault
2. What does Jesus say to do? To love and to pray

3. There is nothing wrong with wanting something, praying for something

4. Don't beat myself up over someone else's choices.

Starting over

I haven't believed in miracles for a long time. Well, that's not true. I believe in miracles for others but not for me. Not that I didn't deserve them but they were never meant for me.

Finding my son was a miracle. One I never expected. One I still can't believe happened.

I will never, ever regret that we connected.

It doesn't matter why it ended. Maybe he pulled away because he felt that he got the information that he was looking for and has no need to move forward.

Or maybe the whole connection was more disruptive than he thought and he didn't want to deal with it.

Or maybe after talking with me and getting to know me, I totally scared him and he couldn't get away fast enough.

None of that matters. He wants nothing more to do with me and so I can only continue to do what I have done the last 39 years. Love him completely and unconditionally. Pray that his life is full of joy and laughter and that he loves and is loved well.

Meanwhile…I continue to focus on getting healthy, with a new understanding and appreciation of where I have been and all that I have come through. I will continue to try and live my life in the moment, soaking up every experience as it comes. The good and the bad. I will continue to share my story in hopes that the next person who is struggling may find a glimmer of hope.

This chapter may be over but my story is not finished. I am picking up the pen and writing the version that I want to live. Praising God for all I have been given and continuing my journey to change the world one dream at a time.

Some days I struggle, some days I am brilliant! (not in the smart way…but in the shining like a star way) but every day, every single day, I choose to be #epic.

About the Author

Jean Tillery is the founder of Epic Living with Jean, a company that offers integrated solutions to the problems that keep people from living their most #epicLife. She is a Certified Dream Manager, the host of #epicStories Podcast, and an Ambassador with Epicure food company.

For years her Dream List included a cross country road trip and after battling many physical and mental struggles, including long Covid, she knew it was time to take her Power of Dreaming Message to the masses and mark that dream off her list.

 The #epicRoadtrip is a project that blends her teaching experience as a home-schooling mom along with her work as a coach, leader, creator, and community builder. She set off on this trip to change people's understanding of dreams and ended up changing her own life in the process.

Milton Keynes UK
Ingram Content Group UK Ltd.
UKHW020243260424
441608UK00006B/85

9 798985 413526